VERTICAL LEAP

Inside The Rise of Tennessee Basketball

DANE BRADSHAW

Foreword by
Coach Bruce Pearl

TENNESSEE VALLEY
Publishing®

2007

Library of Congress Control Number: 2007926563

Published by: Tennessee Valley Publishing
              P.O. Box 52527
              Knoxville, TN 37950
              www.tvp1.com

Printed and bound in the United States of America.

ISBN 978-1-932604-44-3

The front-cover photograph furnished courtesy of Patrick Murphy-Racey, and back-cover photographs furnished courtesy of Elizabeth Olivier of UTSports.com.

Dedicated to my father, Mike Bradshaw

When I was eight years old I had aspirations of writing a book for my father. It turned into more of a letter giving thanks for what he has done for me and the rest of the family. The original still sits on the countertop of his bathroom sink. Excuse the grammatical errors and my attempt at drawing basketballs around the border, I was only eight so cut me some slack....

In many ways, nothing has changed. This book may not be entirely about him, but because of him my life has taken a path that has put me in a position to do something like this. My father has been my greatest fan and supporter while at the same time being my disciplinarian, role model and father in the truest sense. After all the years, it still comes back to "The Man Who Taught Me It All." **Thank You, Dad.**

Acknowledgment

I quickly learned that keeping a journal and entering events into computer text were some of the easier tasks of publishing a book. Fortunately, I found some caring and professional people, who have helped me through the process. Without them, I might simply have a private, personal journal, rather than *Vertical Leap*—a book that documents for *all* of us, an insider's view of our historic 2006-07 basketball campaign.

Craig Pinkerton, head of UT basketball media relations, provided the initial encouragement that reinforced my determination to go ahead with the book project. Craig pointed me to the legendary Haywood Harris, "Historian of the Vols," for advice on publishing. Then, Haywood introduced me to his good friend and published author, Don Ferguson. With no strings attached, Haywood and Don guided me through the entire publishing process. Nothing I could say can articulate my appreciation for their help and expertise. The best people in the world are those who get their greatest pleasure out of helping others; Haywood Harris and Don Ferguson are *the best*. They also led me to Tennessee Valley Publishing, a company best suited to accomplish my book goals.

Margaret and Dwain Kitchel of Tennessee Valley Publishing took my computer notes and with the help of others organized and pulled the book together. Margaret and Dwain are both basketball fans and were pleased to help me finalize and produce *Vertical Leap*. Beyond creating a published book, I have established a great friendship with Margaret and Dwain and am thankful that Haywood and Don led me to Tennessee Valley Publishing.

So, thank you Craig, Don, Haywood and Kitchels for making this book process an enjoyable experience.

Table of Contents

Foreword

When I took the Tennessee job in April of 2005, and met Dane Bradshaw, the first thing I thought is: Where am I going to play him? I knew he wanted to be a point guard, but we didn't really need him there. I also knew he would do anything for the team. That's just the kind of kid he was and the way he was raised. We were so thin inside I needed him every minute I could get at power forward. That's right, a 6'3" starting power forward in the most athletic basketball conference in America, the Southeastern Conference. In hindsight, I have to say it worked out pretty well, a SEC East championship in 2006 and a Sweet 16 appearance in 2007. Only two-time national champions Florida had a better SEC record over those two seasons and we've beaten them three out of the last four meetings.

Dane Bradshaw became a reflection of what I want my Tennessee teams to be. We want to be a pain in your ass. We want to be the team on the schedule that you least look forward to playing, because of how hard our kids play. We want you to look at us in the layup line and go 'No way,' and look at Bradshaw in the layup line and go 'No way.' And then understand, yeah, there is a way and we're going to find it. We're going to beat you with a 6'3" power forward who talks as much trash as Larry Bird.

Dane's got a lot of smack, a lot of confidence. White guys aren't stereotypically known for talking trash, but Dane will talk as much trash as anybody and he'll back it up. He plays with passion and opposing teams can't stand him. He's the white guy who's not very athletic and he's beating up on their All-Americans. But the more they got on him the better he played. I think he got that natural, by growing up in the suburbs of West Tennessee and playing on the inner-city playgrounds of Memphis.

Every person has strengths and weaknesses as it relates to their job. My strength, I think, is my relationship with my players. I try to love them like a father would love a son. I try to expect things of them like a father would expect things of a son. I want them to worry that they'll disappoint me instead of anger me when they miss the mark. Some players are receptive to that. They open the door and let you in and the relationship can be terrifically rewarding. Other players don't need that. They appreciate it, but they don't need it. Dane doesn't need that. He's got the greatest father on earth, the greatest fan, the greatest friend. But he allowed me to come in, to pray with him, to talk to him about himself and his goals, to empower him as a leader. Our relationship has made his redemption, as a player, and this program's resurrection, as a contender, so rewarding. Especially since they took place coincidentally at Tennessee.

Why do we love Dane Bradshaw? We love Dane Bradshaw because he's a great young man. We love him because he's a role model, a terrific student-athlete. He's got God in his life. He's a community servant. He's great with kids at camp. But he was all of those things as a sophomore: a time when most fans didn't know or love him. He wasn't playing the same role then, and he wasn't playing nearly as well. He was here and Florida's Lee Humphrey wasn't. He was the guy who didn't belong, who couldn't play in the SEC and people didn't know him. But he was then, just as he is today, a good young man, a great student, a hard worker, and tough as they come. So one caution I have, even for our amazing fans at Tennessee, is to try not to judge a player or program or even a coach just simply based on winning and losing.

Thankfully, winning in these last couple of years allowed us to appreciate Dane and all the things he was — instead of being critical of all the things he wasn't when we were losing.

I want very much for this time in Tennessee basketball history to be known for something. And if it's for the redemption of Dane Bradshaw and the resurrection of this program, that would be great.

That's why my family and I decided to endow a scholarship in Dane's name. There's an expression, to whom much is given, much is expected. I believe in that. Over these last two years my family has been blessed to finally be in a position where we're financially rewarded. You must do your share to give back. This scholarship helps me forever remind people of this very special time in Tennessee basketball when we got it going again.

Every member of this basketball team the last two years, all the coaches and fans and Mike Hamilton, our athletic director, they all deserve the credit, for making this a special paragraph in the history of Tennessee basketball. We single out Dane Bradshaw, our only senior this year, because he does combine some unique qualities. He's a great student who graduated in three years. He is also a terrific leader. Even in this book, *Vertical Leap*, he's not afraid to tell you about times when he had to say things that needed to be said to another teammate. You can't say it unless you live it and Dane Bradshaw lives it every day of his young life.

Don't call Dane an overachiever. But is there anything wrong with him coming as close as anybody I've coached to maximizing his physical abilities, to take advantage of God's skills he's been given? Dane's very spiritual and I am too. He's not afraid to pray. He's not afraid to cry. He's not afraid to fail. Dane's had my back, on and off the court. I just couldn't let this student-athlete leave without me saying: This is what we're shooting for; this is what we're trying to produce. This scholarship will help do that at a place Dane Bradshaw loves with all his heart, the University of Tennessee.

Being a father of four, I understand how important my kids' teachers are, and how important their youth coaches are. I feel like a parent to every kid who ever played for me, whether I inherited them and they became my players or whether I recruited them and they committed and then signed to come play for me. You accept a tremendous responsibility to do the best job you can for them. To motivate them. To teach them. To counsel them. To support them. To see something in them they don't see in themselves. To be tireless in not allowing them to underachieve in any way, shape or form.

In most cases, we succeed and achieve a great deal together. And in some cases we fail. The failings are the ones who don't graduate or the ones who get sideways with me or with university policy and don't achieve. Those losses hurt worse than losing a 17-point lead to Ohio State to get to the Elite Eight.

So I want to thank Mike and Linda Bradshaw for letting me work with their son. Just like I want to thank all the parents of every player I've ever coached. I ask God every day to give me the wisdom, the patience, the knowledge and the passion to challenge these young men. To take full advantage of the gifts God has bestowed upon them. To honor God and their families every day with their actions, not just their words. To deserve victory, as we prepare them for life after basketball and that *vertical leap*.

Coach Bruce Pearl
April 2007

Introduction

Under Coach Bruce Pearl's leadership, there has been a major rebirth in the vitality, competitiveness and popularity of the University of Tennessee's men's basketball team. As the lone senior, I have been fortunate to have played a role in the turn around of the program. With UT fan interest at an all-time high, I felt like it was an excellent time to write about the team from a player's perspective.

Being a fan myself, I know how enjoyable it is to cheer for a team, and I understand how attached one can become to his or her team. However, as a fan, you are usually on the outside looking in and must rely heavily on the media for information. By keeping a journal throughout the season, I felt that I could then write a book that would provide an insider's view that fans would enjoy on a more personal level.

During the summer of 2006, I approached Coach Pearl about writing such a book. I not only believed the timing was right; I had just begun the road to recovery from wrist surgery and felt I could successfully accomplish the project. Coach was encouraging and directed me to Craig Pinkerton—head of basketball media relations.

I called Craig, whom we call "Pink." Before I could finish explaining my idea, Pink cut me off and said, "Do it." He said that when he worked at the University of Kansas a player did something similar and was very successful. With this positive response to my idea, I began writing a recap of the summer sessions and started my day-to-day journal entries. Throughout the day, I would simply make notes that I thought would be of interest. These notes became the foundation of this book.

Our first official game of the season was against Middle Tennessee State University on November 10, 2006. However, for many of us the season began months before November 10. Soon after the March Madness hurrahs end, preparation for the new season begins. Coaches and players do everything within their power to get an edge up, hoping to be a part of the last team standing in the season to follow. So my behind-the-scenes coverage starts long before our first official game and is organized into three major sections: Preseason Preparation (April 2006 to November 9, 2006), Season Play (November 10, 2006 to March 3, 2007) and Postseason Play (March 8, 2007 to March 22, 2007).

My goal is to take you with me as we capture the entirety of our basketball season. Hopefully, this will help develop an even greater appreciation and bond between fans and players. Conditioning, practice, games, competitors, fans, family, coaches, teammates, media, and balancing school, basketball and personal lives are subjects I discuss, using my own observations and interpretations.

For me it's been an unbelievable ride. Thank you and welcome to our season through my eyes.

Section I — Preseason Preparation

Wrist Injury

B asketball is supposedly a noncontact sport, with game officials dedicated to enforcing that aspect of the game. But as any fan or player knows, the close proximity of ten players, the athletic movements involved and the fast pace of the game results in significant contact between players and gym floors. As a result, scraped and skinned body parts, bruises, and sprains are everyday fare for the players. And the potential for more significant injuries is always present.

Unfortunately, I was tagged with a serious wrist injury during UT's 2005-06 basketball season. This injury has had such an impact on my play and our team, including far too much media attention, that I felt compelled to share some details and effects of the injury. While this injury is my story, these types of injuries are commonplace in sports, and my story illustrates what a lot of college athletes must endure for the love of playing their sport.

On January 21, 2006, our team was facing its first losing streak of the season. We had lost back-to-back games for the first time and were hosting Florida at home. With a win, Florida would become the number-one ranked team in the country. Excitement was in the air and our gym at Thompson-Boling Arena was sold out. I won't discuss the entire game but it was a classic that turned out to be a key victory for UT. It gained us legitimate respect in the basketball world and provided yet another spark in our fan and student support.

My injury occurred about midway through the second half. The ball was passed in to Florida's Chris Richard and I moved over to help a teammate. I put my right hand onto the ball before

Richard was able to get the ball off for a shot and thought I was going to force a jump ball situation. With my hand on the ball, Richard continued to bring the ball up to shoot and with his enormous strength turned my wrist in an awkward direction.

I was called for a foul and immediately felt a sharp pain in my wrist. I gave the standard pissed-off look at the referee because I really felt I had "all ball" and the call should have been a jump ball. Nevertheless, a foul was called. I couldn't wait for a timeout because I knew I needed some tape. My wrist was taped quickly and I got back into the game, where right away I was fouled. At the time I didn't know I had torn a ligament, but there I am shooting a free throw in front of 25,000 fans. I knew I was in pain, but had no idea how this was going to affect my shooting. When I released the free throw, I knew the ball was shot way too short. The ball barely grazed the front of the rim. I tried to act mad at the miss, but I was actually giving thanks that I didn't airball the free throw.

Anyway, we won the game with Chris Lofton making a remarkable steal and throwing it ahead to me for the game-winning layup. For those who wondered why I was at the other end of the court and not getting back on defense, it was because I had just fallen down trying to get a rebound and had trouble getting up with one hand. Then I'm rewarded with the easiest game-winning shot you will ever see! If that's not divine intervention, I don't know what is!

After the game and celebration, I stayed in the training room to have my wrist examined by our team doctor and our trainer, Dr. Val Gene Iven and Chad Newman. The wrist was wrapped with ice and they gave me some anti-inflammatories and told me that we would have it X-rayed as soon as possible. I assumed it was a bad sprain, but when I got in my car and tried to turn the key in the ignition; the pain was awful. That's when I realized something more serious was wrong. Also, trying to zip up my pants or put my belt on or any other simple activity caused severe pain. Still, I kept hoping that it was just a sprain.

When the X-rays were taken, they came back negative, which was not a surprise to me because I didn't feel like I had broken anything. Our plan was to wait and see how the wrist reacted after a week or so. The pain lessened a little bit but not much, and Chad continued to try different taping techniques that could help me play. I continued to play with the wrist heavily taped and the pain stayed about the same.

Since the pain didn't go away, the wrist was once again X-rayed. As I suspected, the results were again negative. Dr. Iven told me the continued pain plus other factors led him to believe there was a tear. I didn't want to hear bad news, so I took his comments as a worst-case scenario and, for my own peace of mind, tried to ignore them. We finally scheduled an MRI, which rarely brings good news.

The MRI was done the day before we hit the road to face the Kentucky Wildcats. I wouldn't find out the results until after the Kentucky game. We won that game with Chris Lofton putting on one of the most unbelievable, clutch performances I have ever seen. I only scored two points but that was one of the most memorable wins of my life.

Not too many basketball teams can say they have won at Rupp Arena, and we did just that as our dream season continued. I'm sure most readers are familiar with the "Hulk Hogan imitation" that Coach Pearl did in the locker room. It was on the postseason DVD, and I was the first one to wrap my arms around Coach Pearl. My Mom saw that scene on the DVD and told me that it was one of the happiest looks she had ever seen on my face.

When we returned to Knoxville, the team was riding high. It was fun to walk on campus. We players actually didn't mind going to class because of the love and support we were receiving from our classmates and friends.

After class I went to the Knoxville Orthopedic Clinic (KOC) to find out the results of my MRI. Chad Newman was going to meet me there for my appointment with Dr. Robert Ivy. I called Chad, who was already at KOC, and said, "I think it feels a little better today." Dr. Ivy explained the MRI results to me. He told me that I had torn the main wrist ligament, and that a person can have a partial tear, a 50 percent tear, a 75 percent tear, etc. I remember his exact words, "What you have is a 100 percent tear."

The explanation got harder to handle as he went on, and the implications became clearer to me. He told me that as a doctor it was his job to advise me to have surgery right away to repair the ligament while the tissue was still fresh. The longer you wait to have surgery the harder it is to repair a ligament, and by delaying the surgery your future in basketball could be jeopardized. At this point I bit my tongue and tried my best to keep my composure. I thought I was prepared to hear the worst, but now I have a doctor advising me to have surgery and end this dream season or possibly never be able to play the game that has been the focus of my life since I was about four years old. It is the doctor's job to give you the best advice and inform you of the worst-case scenario. Dr. Ivy said for me to discuss my situation with Chad, the coaching staff, and my family. He then left the room so that Chad and I could talk. That's when I lost it. I mean I broke down and cried. Chad put his arms around me as I wept.

In the last twelve hours, I had gone through a roller-coaster change of emotions. I went from the peak of happiness, that my mother described as one of the happiest expressions of my life, to an abyss of tears. I knew there was no way I would have the surgery until after the basketball season, but it scared the hell out of me. It was not a difficult decision for me to make, just a hard decision to deal with.

Dr. Ivy came back in the room and I made it clear that I would not have surgery until after the season, but he told me to take sometime to make the decision and discuss it with my parents once my emotions calmed down. Dr. Ivy could not have been more professional, caring, and supportive. I was fortunate to be around such kind people as Dr. Ivy and Chad.

I left the office past the nurses with my teary-eyed face and could feel them looking at me with sympathy. Actually, it was embarrassing. I sent a text message to Mom asking her to call Chad because I really couldn't talk at the time. I thought I had gathered my emotions and called Julia, my girlfriend, but immediately choked up as I started to tell her the news. Later I called my brother and broke down again. I don't know why, but as soon as I would start talking about my problem I would get overly emotional. Eventually I was able to have a conversation with my parents. They told me that if I wanted to have the surgery I had nothing to be ashamed of, because I had already shown my toughness and had nothing to prove. My parents said all the right things, but they knew as well as I did that there was no way of keeping me off the court. Coach Pearl also was very supportive and never put pressure on me to play. He talked with my parents and the doctors about it and showed compassion toward me. It was obvious that Coach's major concern was for me as a person. My health and future were more important to him than anything I could do to help the UT basketball team.

We continued to ice the wrist and tried to stay away from any unnecessary contact. Chad would tape it up heavily before each practice and game. Many times he would tape it up and ask, "How does that feel?" I would look down at my hand turning purple from lack of circulation and reply, "Perfect, can't feel a thing. Thanks."

We decided to keep the injury from the media until the end of the season, so it wouldn't be a distraction. Then Dave Odom, head coach of South Carolina, spilled the beans at the SEC Tournament. After South Carolina eliminated us, Coach Odom asked me about the wrist and I informed him I would be having surgery after the season. Coach Odom was praising my efforts to the media after the game, and he told them I was going to have surgery. Then, he immediately apologized for exposing that to the media. It really was not a big deal; it was going to happen at some point anyway.

I played with the injured wrist from January 21, 2006, until our loss to Wichita State in mid-March. I would never have said so at the time, but it really did begin to wear and I know it affected the little things I provided on the court. My steals, rebounds, and other stats decreased. I just couldn't be as aggressive or strong with the hand as I once was. Many people applauded my efforts to continue playing. But I don't see how any player, given the choice, could end the unbelievable season we were having, because nothing is promised next year. When my teammates would ask how it was feeling, I would joke by saying, "It hurts like hell, but I'm playing through it so I can get an article in the newspaper about it."

A few days after our season-ending loss to Wichita State, I had the surgery. My mom was told about an extraordinary wrist doctor in Indianapolis named Dr. Art Rettig—the Colts' team surgeon. Dr. Rettig is one of the top wrist surgeons in the nation. When mom heard that he was available, there was no changing her mind.

The surgery was successful and Dr. Rettig was pleased with the way things went. Pins were put in my wrist to help reattach the ligament. Dr. Rettig was as nice as could be and did not possess the arrogance you might think a renowned surgeon would have. I was in a soft cast for a week before being put in a hard cast for eight more weeks. Then I had a small surgery to remove the pins and had one more week in a soft cast. Finally, that cast was off and my arm was free. I had the absolute greatest tan line of all time. To make things worse, they shaved my arm for surgery and my arm hair grew back extremely dark and thick. I resembled Teen Wolf.

Rehabilitation began and consisted of me trying to move my hand slightly up and down, side to side. It was discouraging at first, but I stayed dedicated to my rehab. The wrist improved slowly but surely. The injury is a six-month injury. I have seen it referred to as the "ACL to the wrist." It wasn't a process you could just tough out or be extremely aggressive with because that would just cause swelling. My patience was tested every day. I went back and forth to Indianapolis about five times for checkups with Dr. Rettig. The wrist progressed the way he wanted, and on a visit in early July he gave me some unexpected news. I didn't think I would be cleared to shoot or play until August, but he was so pleased with my progress that he cleared me to start shooting basketballs. He told me to start with about twenty shots a day and to shoot no farther than the free throw line. This may sound insignificant, but to a basketball junkie who hasn't shot a basketball in about four-and-a-half months it was groundbreaking news. I started shooting that day. It hurt but I was happy to be doing it. This was a lot of fun for someone who has had to do left-handed drills for all of June. The wrist brace still had to be worn while shooting, but I had been wearing something on my wrist for seven months so that was nothing. This excited me and gave me new goals heading into the second session of summer.

So for all who have been nice enough to ask about my wrist, this is the lengthy answer. Now I can turn to the book's purpose—our team activities, from an insider's perspective.

Summer Session 1 Recap

As the month of June rolls around, most of the players report to summer school and get back to working out on a regular basis. This year, more than ever, the spotlight is on our much-heralded freshman class. I have seen the class ranked as high as number three in the nation. We are all happy to bring in more talent to help the team improve, but this makes the returning players look over their shoulders and worry about playing time. When asked about the incoming freshmen, we continue to give politically correct answers by saying something like, "I'm really excited about having so many great players coming in; I think they will help us right away." Yeah right, that sounds good, but each of us is competing for playing time and now we have to compete against the nation's number-three recruiting class. The class consists of point guards, shooting guards, forwards, and centers. To make matters worse they can all play multiple positions. I know this sounds selfish, but, from a player's viewpoint, it's a reality. And I am writing this book to provide personal thoughts and behind-the-scene stories, which go beyond quotes and information presented in the media.

Each player has personal goals in basketball, and it would be a lot easier to accomplish those goals if there were fewer people to compete against. But to have a great team it can't be that way. I am not as worried about the recruits as some of the other returning players. That is not to say that I feel as though my playing time is safe, but I am far enough along in my basketball-playing career to understand that we all gain by having better players and a better team. Just like any other player, I would love to be the star of the team, but I realize how close I am to being part of the most successful team in the University's history.

A huge part of unselfishness is being able to balance personal goals and team goals. Trouble begins when individual aspirations have higher priorities than team goals. Players need to understand that the more successful the entire team is, the more each individual will benefit. I believe that we have team members who will buy into that concept.

We remember how much fun we had last year with our winning season. But few people realize that we were one win away from arguably being the best team in the school's history. You may think I'm crazy to say that, but only one University of Tennessee team has gone to the Sweet 16, since the field expanded to 64 teams. In the past, notwithstanding the talent that has played at UT, postseason success has not been a strong suit. So, as shorthanded as we were last year, if we don't screw up against Wichita State we are in the Sweet 16! How can you not make a point that we were one of the greatest teams in the school's history? For team comparisons, see Table 1 page 184.

This brings me back to the freshmen. Surely I can sacrifice a few minutes of playing time and some of the spotlight in exchange for being part of the greatest team in UT history. The freshmen, along with the individual improvements of our returning players, can help us get to the next level and possibly make this next season historic. I welcome the new players....as long as they don't take too much of my playing time.

Wayne Chism and Marques Johnson are the only two freshmen who came to the first session of summer school. The others were expected to report in July. The transition to University life is always tough for a freshman. One of the big issues for me was laundry. In the mornings, I would pick a shirt off the floor and take a sniff. If it smelled fine, then great. If it smelled bad, I would grab another shirt. Right? No, I would grab a bottle of Febreeze and give the shirt a few sprays and off I would go. It didn't matter if my shorts smelled awful because you could get away with that. Each set of boxers and socks were good for at least a week and a half. I have gotten better with the laundry situation, a.k.a., I got a girlfriend. That helps a great deal.

Time management may be one of the hardest transitions for a student-athlete. You must wake up in time for 7:30 a.m. weight workouts, a workout that a freshman can't possibly be prepared to do. Then you rush out of the weight room drenched in sweat, grab your books and hustle off to class, starting at around 9:30 a.m. There is rarely time to take a shower before class. Class gets out around 11 a.m. and you walk (usually more like a painful limp as a result of morning workouts) to your next class at around 11:30 a.m. Finally, you're done with class. Now you have to grab a quick bite because you have to hurry to the Thornton Center for tutoring assistance. After this, you may be able to get a thirty-minute rest in before the 4 p.m. workouts. These workouts are "voluntary," but you know your butt had better be there. By the end of the "voluntary" workouts, you have been going from 7:30 a.m. to 5:30 p.m. Sounds like an overload, but I believe the coaching staff's thought process is that the busier the kid is the more focused he has to be. If all you have time for is basketball and school then your mission is accomplished. After all these are the two major reasons we're here.

My schedule is not nearly as bad as my teammates' schedules. Because I graduated early, finishing last spring, I have no summer classes to take. I work out in the morning with the guys and as they go off to class I politely tell them, "Have a great day at class; I'm going home to take a nap and watch *The Price is Right*." We take great delight in kidding each other, including rubbing in what few advantages we have. However, I spent most of my days doing wrist rehabilitation (rehab).

After surgery to repair a ligament in late March, I finally got the cast off but still have a brace and cannot do anything other than my rehab stretches with that hand. The cast really set my conditioning back because I was not allowed to do any running for the 10 weeks I had it on. My right arm has the definition of an average 80-year-old woman's arm.

I remember how excited I was when the doctor cleared me to run. I went straight to the track and, of course, decided to get back in shape in one day. This was not the smartest decision I have ever made. No one could tell macho me that I needed to take it slow. I was ready to get back in shape right away.

I arrive at the track and saw a few people in the bleachers, but I pay them little mind. I stretch out and set my stopwatch, getting ready to run a six-minute mile. I take off and the first lap feels very good. Half way through the second lap, I'm breathing very hard, and it goes downhill from there. I barely make it to the end of the second lap before having to stop and hit the ground. I'm gasping as hard as you can imagine, spitting all over the place and then here come leg cramps. The stopwatch has not yet reached three minutes and I am laid out, spitting up everything, and trying to stretch my cramps.

As if my pride was not hurt enough, I hear some quiet laughter. I forgot there were people sitting in the stands who just witnessed one of the worst attempts at being an athlete. It was an embarrassing moment for me, and I'm sure I left them with high expectations for Tennessee's upcoming basketball season.

Back to Wayne Chism and Marques Johnson, no one could have picked better teammates. They work extremely hard on and off the court, they are on time, and get along with everyone. A great thing about these two is they push everyone else. I'm not just saying this on a talent level, but on a work ethic level. As an upperclassman, when you look over and see an incoming freshman pushing himself and getting up extra shots, it makes you say, "I can't let this freshman outwork me." For a team, this is a huge positive motivation—pushing each other and making each other better. Hopefully, this type of work ethic and attitude will continue for all of us.

As for me, it continued to be tough to watch everyone else play basketball while I sat on the sidelines doing left-handed ball handling. The good thing is that I could focus primarily on my conditioning and foot speed. Graduating in three years was a blessing in disguise, because it allowed me time in June to focus on wrist rehab and getting back into shape rather than having to take classes.

Although we had two great additions in Marques and Wayne, we lost a player that we expected and wanted to return. One of the team's favorites, Damion Harris, will not be back. He red-shirted last season and his body control and strength made tremendous improvements. However, his on-court development and conditioning still needed some work before he would have a legitimate shot at getting significant playing time for the team. Damion is a player who, when developed, could really impact the game with his size alone. I hope he finds the right school that can fully use his talents. Like I said, he was a team favorite and a friend who gave me one of the funniest memories of my career.

Ironically, this story came immediately after a tough loss to Arkansas at home where we blew a sizeable lead. We are back in the locker room sitting in silence with our chairs circled around Coach Pearl. Coach will rub his face and let a loss soak in without saying a word, but we have learned to be prepared for a loud outburst at anytime. I don't say this lightly, because he can yell at anytime and it will scare the hell out of you. Chris Lofton once jumped so high in his seat it was like he was watching *Friday the 13th*.

Anyway, Coach goes on his rampage with his face red, veins on his neck popping out, and spit hanging off his bottom lip. For some reason before the game we had a bowl of oranges for the players in the locker room. Unfortunately, there were plenty of oranges left and the bowl was still in the center of the locker room. I'm looking at Coach, then looking at the bowl. I'm anticipating the direction in which the oranges will be kicked, because at this point it's not "if," it's more a matter of "where" the oranges are going to be kicked. **"We do not get outworked!"** Coach Pearl screams. Here it comes, BOOM! Pearl kicked the bowl of oranges like it was the final penalty kick for the World Cup. The oranges hit Damion Harris directly in the face. The juice and pulp are running down Damion's cheeks and he has the most hilarious expression on his face. I have never been so mad about a loss and had my emotions flip into uncontrollable laughter so quickly. Damion is trying his best to keep a stern, serious face while listening to Coach, and he is too scared or stunned to wipe the pulp, peels and seeds from his face. You have to realize that Damion is a red-shirt and did not get to play last year, so he has had nothing to do with the outcome of the game. Yet he is the victim of the Tropicana Assassin. In the next couple of minutes his face goes from dripping to just stickiness, and a seed dangles from his chin hair. I cannot stop looking at Damion even though I'm worried that I will burst into laughter during Coach's rant. Finally, in the middle of his tantrum, Coach says, "Sorry Damion." This was a message that told Damion he could wipe his face off. I think Coach waited a while to see if Damion would react negatively to the oranges on his face, because that would have given Coach more ammunition to be angry. But Damion passed the orange-bombardment test.

The coaching staff leaves and we wait a second to make sure it's clear, so we can laugh quietly with Damion. It was one of those stories that would get told over and over again throughout the season and never got old. I wish Damion the best and none of us will forget that moment.

Damion's departure leads me to Major Wingate. It is publicly known that Major was suspended from the team indefinitely. Major has been working hard in the classroom and on the court to get back in the coaching staff's good graces. A suspension is a very serious thing and I do not want to downplay it, but it does not include all the harsh punishments many people think. You are watched and monitored closely, but I feel like a suspension is more like a final warning rather than a huge punishment. Major is one of those guys who is just cool with everyone. At 6'10" 245 pounds, it is easy for the average person to be intimidated by his presence alone. But Major goes out of his way to be nice to everyone he meets, and many would be surprised at his kindness, because he has such a dominating stature. I hope Major can get through this suspension and have his best season yet, but I wish I could be more sure that history won't repeat itself.

When a player gets into trouble off the court, it is likely to be front page news for local newspapers. Once a player gets into trouble there are constant reports on his status that continue to remind people of his problems. In other words, it never really goes away. Coach Pearl raises a pertinent question when he asks, "Does the punishment fit the crime?" It is difficult to regain a good reputation, because there are constant reminders to the public about past misdeeds. For example, after a game a columnist may write, "Player A, who was arrested last season, made the game winning basket." The legal part had absolutely nothing to do with the game, but it is just another way to remind people that the player has had problems in the past.

My main point in discussing this kind of situation is to show how hard it is to recover from a damaged reputation and how important it is to try to stay out of trouble, especially as an athlete. In a college atmosphere, you really have to focus on thinking before acting because there are so many people, places and things that can lead to trouble. All it takes is one screw-up before your career is in jeopardy. Coach Pearl often warns us of such situations and tells us to ask ourselves, "Is it really worth it?"

On a lighter note, Coach Pearl's basketball camp was in action, and the attendance was almost quadrupled from last summer. It was exciting to see the look on these kids' faces when we came around. We know we are heroes in their eyes. The fun part is remembering that when I was their age I had those same feelings. My number 23 jersey is now for sale, which is one of the coolest things to me. I say this in a very humble way. I know my jersey is not a top-selling product and that my parents' credit card is used for most of the sales, but it is still cool to me.

At camp there was a kid with my jersey on and he comes up to me and says "Watch this!" He grabs a camp ball and throws it into the middle of the court and chases after it, then spins and lays it up in the basket while shouting, "Florida throws it in, Bradshaw with the steal. Oh! He spins and lays it up! It's good. Tennessee wins the game!" He then proceeds to celebrate and dance around by himself before coming up to me and saying, "That's what you did, right?" To see a camper wearing my jersey, imagining he was me, and imitating winning the Florida game was touching to me. I used to be his age pretending to be Scottie Pippen for the Bulls. Now don't think I am trying to compare my basketball skills to those of Scottie Pippen.

Scottie Pippen Basketball Camp

I do try my best to be as nice as possible to the kids. Whether it is signing a pair of my old game shoes and giving them away or just carrying on a small conversation, I enjoy trying to make their day. I have a little extra motivation in being nice to kids. Scottie Pippen was a childhood hero of mine. When I was about 11 years old, I found out about the Scottie Pippen Basketball Camp in Conway, Arkansas. My parents drove me from Memphis to Conway for the camp of my dreams. There, I am finally going to meet the man whose posters and memorabilia cover my room from end to end.

The camp begins and Pippen is not there, but we campers give him the benefit of the doubt and assume he is busy. Finally the day comes when we are scheduled to have Pippen come around to all the dorm rooms to meet us. I am freaking out on whether to wear my Pippen jersey or my Chicago Bulls T-shirt. This is a big decision; I wanted to be accepted by Scottie Pippen. Scottie walks through our door and I am about overcome with excitement and nervousness. I mean he is a god to me! I shake his hand and he shakes my roommate's hand, and before I can get a word out he says, "All right what do you want me to sign? I have to hurry; there are a lot of kids to get to." I take my little picture and he leaves. Are you kidding me? That was it? No, "Thanks for coming to my camp," or even just a "Where are you from?" Anything! He could have said anything in a nice way directed toward me and I would have continued to be his fan, but he didn't. So, after he left, we got together and compared our brief Pippen meetings. This bunch of eager young kids who didn't know how to cuss quickly turned into a group of foulmouthed 11 year olds, screaming "F*** Scottie Pippen!" It's amusing now, but it was a minor tragedy for us.

To make things worse, Pippen planned to be present at the end of camp to hand out awards. So I believed there was still hope; maybe if I win MVP we can have a nice conversation. Long story short, I win MVP but Scottie F'n Pippen took an early flight back to Chicago and I receive my MVP award from the Central Arkansas assistant coach. Wow!

My parents come to pick me up and because I am silent Mom can tell something is wrong. But I got MVP, what could be the problem? I walk to the car, put my bag in and throw my stupid trophy in the back and yell, "I hate Scottie Pippen." When we get home, I rip down every Pippen poster.

I probably expected too much of Pippen's time and have since forgiven him, which I'm sure is a huge load off his mind. Because of this experience, I promised myself to try to be the nicest, most grateful and enthusiastic guy, if I was ever put in a similar situation. This is why I try my best to let my fans (especially kids) know how much I appreciate them.

Summer Pickup Games

When camp ends for the day, it is time for the players to play some pickup. For those unfamiliar with basketball terminology, pickup is just guys playing 5-on-5 full court. It often gets sloppy and selfish, but that's just how pickup is played. Pearl tells us that summer is the time to be selfish in terms of focusing on bettering yourself and your game. Pickup games can get really competitive, and they can be a lot of fun, particularly when some of the old UT players come back and play with us.

Ron Slay and Isiah Victor were two big names who joined in some of our pickup games. I am still not allowed to play because of my wrist, but it was fun to watch. No one talks more trash than Ron Slay. There was a funny incident between Slay and Ryan Childress back in the summer of '05 when Childress was an incoming freshman. Slay was a chubby guy who looks older than his age. Well, Ryan has no idea who this guy is and he didn't really like the way Slay was running his mouth. So he decides to talk some trash back. Keep in mind, you have former All-American and SEC Player of the Year, Ron Slay, competing with an unproven incoming freshman—Ryan Childress. Ryan proceeds to tell Slay what a fat old man he is and to take his ass back to the rec. league. Needless to say Slay won the matchup. And, as he said, "Teach this young white boy a lesson." We informed Ryan after the game who he was dealing with and his reply was, "Really? Yeah he was pretty good, so what?"

I tell you this story because we basically had a repeat this summer between Wayne Chism and Isiah Victor. Wayne didn't know and didn't care who Victor was and the two went at it. Victor would repeatedly, after each bucket, tell Wayne to "respect yo elders, boy." In the end Chism won the matchup because of his strength. But it was funny how these young freshmen came in and showed complete disrespect for two of the best players in UT's history—Victor and Slay. It did make the games better and everyone shook hands when it was all said and done. Victor and Slay are both great guys and everyone loves it when they come back.

Team Chemistry

With so many new players coming in, some people have wondered about the team's chemistry. I can honestly say that after the first summer session, this is the closest a team has been since I arrived at UT. Never before have so many of us hung out together so often off the court. Especially during the NBA playoffs, almost every game, a group of us would get together. This is after we've been around each other since 7:30 a.m. This shows we don't get tired of each other and that the team is bonding more than ever. Last year we had more guys who were loners and were more interested in doing their own thing. Of course this was fine because we all need our own time away from the team. But we never hung out as a team unless it was a function at Coach Pearl's house or some other team-structured event.

But this summer, we have a much closer-knit team. After workouts in the afternoon, we may all go get something to eat. On the weekends I get calls from almost every player to see what's going on for the night. This may not sound like a big deal, but it's something I think is important and will benefit us in the long run. We are all working extremely hard and have common goals. The great thing is we try to kick each other's butts through workouts; then go hang out right afterwards.

We understand each other and I hope we can have this same kind of bonding experience with the other newcomers reporting in July. This excites me as much as anything because I want to enjoy my last collegiate year with a close group of friends. This is no disrespect of my earlier UT teammates and friends; it's just that from a team standpoint, I haven't felt like I was part of such a close team since my high school days.

Summer Session 2 Recap

After a fourth of July break it is nice to get back to workouts. Josh Tabb, a guard from Illinois, and Duke Crews, a 6'7" forward and the most talked about recruit of the class, arrived for summer school. They went through the same adjustments as Marques and Wayne did. It is a growing-up process when you go away to college. I told Duke how important it was to get off to a good start, because it helps to gain the trust of the coaching staff. Otherwise, they will check every class and constantly be into your business, which can be overwhelming and annoying.

One day Duke and I were having a casual conversation about the recruiting process. It amazed me when he spoke of visits with Coach K and Roy Williams, yet he chose Tennessee. It shows how quickly Coach Pearl and his staff are impacting the college basketball scene. If Coach Pearl can get a recruit over North Carolina and Duke after just one season, I can't wait to see what will happen in the future. The coaching staff has always recruited well, but now our winning has raised the bar and the sky is the limit. One problem with recruiting a great player like Duke is, the media can hype it, as if he is the savior of UT basketball. This isn't to say he won't be, but it is better to be patient and let an incredible athlete like Duke have a little time to develop his skills and confidence. There is no question he is a great addition to the team, but I believe it may take awhile before he truly blossoms into the player the people, including Duke himself, want to see. I think he will already be a force in the SEC, so it is scary when I say he has room to improve. There is no question that he will become a crowd favorite after the fans see one of his high-flying dunks. The kids will go crazy over him. Not to mention his name, Duke Crews, is fitting for a star. Already, I can hear the fans shouting, "DUUUUUUKKKKKEE!" in the same tone they shout for Coach Pearl with, "BRRRRUUUUCCCEEEE!" Duke is worth the excitement and I'm looking forward to being his teammate, but everyone needs to realize he is a freshman and be patient with his development. His greatness almost surely will come.

Josh Tabb has become a close friend. He came with a hurt wrist and ended up having a fracture which required surgery; then he was in a cast for a month. We all joked that he knew it was broken, and he just waited until he came to UT so the school would pay for it. Josh swears he didn't know and I believe him. We were just joshing him in a good-humored way. He is one of those guys who is funny without meaning to be. He came from a prep school, so coming to college for him was like escaping jail. The day I gave him my number and told him to call me, he called me nonstop. I realized he was stuck in his Gibbs dorm room with nothing to do and didn't know anyone.

My girlfriend was having a party at her house that night and there was going to be a band in the backyard. I knew it was going to be a lot of fun. I wasn't sure how Josh felt about going to my girl's party, but I called him and told him my plan for the night. He said, "I don't care where I go, I just want to go somewhere." I told him I would pick him up from Gibbs in about thirty minutes. Before I got off the phone Josh says, "Wait, if it's a lil' white party, should I like wear some preppie type shirt?" I started laughing and told him to wear whatever he wanted and not to worry about it; just be himself. When I pick him up, he comes walking to the car wearing baggy jean shorts with a long T-shirt that read, "Hello, I AM A PIMP." I am laughing my ass off. He went from a nice collared shirt to "I AM A PIMP." We arrive at the party and everything is cool, the band is playing, and I introduce Josh to some people and they seem to be having an all right time. Later on, I couldn't find Josh. If I take a teammate to a party, I try to make sure he is having a good time. Well, I look for Josh to see if he is OK or bored and I found him playing drums with the band. Josh freaking Tabb! I'm worried about him being bored, while he is the life of the party trying to learn to play the drums in his I AM A PIMP T-shirt. I took a picture and didn't worry about Josh for the rest of night. He was doing just fine without me. Josh can get along with anyone. Josh and I believe we can adapt to most environments, because we get along with different types of people.

As far as workouts are concerned, they got a little tougher. Troy Wills, our strength coach, has focused a lot on straight line running and speed mechanics. We work on not having any false steps, which in turn can make our running and defense more efficient. Of course we focus a great deal on getting stronger, too. Troy does an amazing job and is constantly thinking of ways to get us better. He doesn't just make things up to kick our asses. He finds ways to help us improve. Now, that usually includes kicking our asses, but that isn't his main objective. Coach Pearl asked Troy to start putting in a little more conditioning into the workouts because he felt the pickup games weren't enough. Coach Pearl knows that summer is not the time to be at the peak of your conditioning because you will wear down in the season. But Coach felt like we needed a little more conditioning at this time.

The thought of more conditioning struck fear into us because there is no telling what Troy will invent. Friday became the hard conditioning day. The first conditioning Friday was brutal. We have this machine called Jacob's Ladder. It is hard to explain, but you strap a belt around your waist and run up a ladder in an inclined position, similar to a StairMaster. Troy has us sprint on the Jacob's Ladder, which records distance and time, for 100 feet. This requires a constant sprint and leg drive for about 30-40 seconds. Then you go straight to whatever weight exercise Troy has scheduled. An example would be Jacob's Ladder, dumbbell bench, and back to Jacob's Ladder. So, after each weight exercise, you have to sprint up the Jacob's Ladder for 100 feet. This went on, with no breaks, until each person had done 700 feet of the ladder. It may not sound tough, but our legs were shaking and some of us were getting a little lightheaded. As soon as we thought we were done, Troy says, "Come out to the field, we are doing defensive slides." This is when everyone begins cursing out of frustration. But Troy shows his compassion by telling us, "You will pass out before you die. Let's go." What? Are you kidding me, Troy? People can hardly walk, not to mention walk-on Ben Bosse has just puked his guts out in a trash can, and our motivational words are, "You will pass out before you die." Well that's encouraging, thanks Troy. I'm not sure that made sense, but Troy knew we could fight through it and we did. Afterwards, we all laid out over the field as if a bomb had just hit and randomly dispersed our dead bodies across the field.

Troy is very intelligent, but he can be an unconventional "meathead," who seems to care very little what others think about his approach to solving a problem. At times, the "meathead" in him can appear. For example, Troy and I had finished a Saturday morning work out and both had some errands to run in west Knoxville, so we drove there together. Troy had this idea for the weight room which required a piece of dowel (a round piece of wood in various lengths). Basically, his idea was to do a lunge type exercise while holding the dowel behind his neck. It's really a good idea, but he gets so into it. We are in Lowe's and Troy has this long piece of dowel behind his neck doing lunges up and down the aisle while saying, "Oh yeah, that's good. That really fires through the glutes." Meanwhile, I am monitoring the aisles as people try to walk by this dude doing lunges with this cylindrically shaped piece of wood. You have to know Troy. He was there to get a piece of dowel, and he was going to see if it worked, no matter that other Lowe's customers might think he was more than a little strange. The guy is an amazing strength coach. His job to improve UT athletes is difficult, because he must deal with so many different personalities. There are the tough guys who can do whatever he says, and then there are guys who just try to get by. He knows when he really needs to get after people and push while maintaining respect between himself and the athlete. He will completely tear us apart, but after the workout we want to stay and chill out with him. He has special leadership qualities that allow him to earn the respect of players even while being very demanding.

The coaches have been on the road recruiting for most of the summer. All the coaches are extremely busy and dedicated, but Coach Pearl never seems to stop. He is on the road more than he would like to be. And, when he is in town, he is often speaking at some function. He is constantly working and trying his best to promote the basketball program. Many have advised him to cut down on some of his special events, but he wants to help out everybody he can.

For instance, he was in town to help wrap up the last basketball camp of the summer and was on his way home for his son's birthday party. En route to his house, he received a phone call from the women's soccer coach asking him to meet one of their top recruits who was on campus. Coach Pearl turns the car around and heads back to the gym to meet the recruit. He calls us over to meet the young girl, and goes above and beyond any standard of duty to help recruit this player for soccer. We all know how convincing and entertaining Coach Pearl is, and he gave this young soccer player the same treatment he would have given a top basketball recruit. This had to impress the young lady and was probably the thing she talked about most when she returned home. The point is Coach Pearl wants the best for the University of Tennessee, not just his team, and does all he can do to help the university. I think he is helping build a closer bond among all the coaches at the university and increasing mutual support between sports.

His unselfishness and down-to-earth demeanor are remarkable. A key reason is he knows how it feels when you aren't at the top. Coach was never spoon fed. He worked his way up through the coaching ranks by years of dedicated and successful service. He has told me how appreciative he was when important coaches gave him their time and advice when he wasn't well known. At the NCAA Tournament in his last year at University of Wisconsin-Milwaukee (UWM), Coach Pearl's team was preparing for the second round of the tournament, and a win against Alabama would give them a Sweet 16 berth. In a conversation between Coach Pearl and Mark Gottfried, head coach of Alabama, Coach Gottfried asked Pearl something like, "How are you going to break through and get a high major coaching job?" Coach Pearl's reply was "Well, I'm going to beat you Mark." I'm sure he said it in a humorous way, because he would never try and be disrespectful to another individual. Sure enough, UWM beats Alabama and becomes the Cinderella team of the tournament, which leads to his job offer from the University of Tennessee. He is an amazing coach, and I am fortunate to be part of the Pearl Era at Tennessee.

While Coach Pearl was in town for camp, I approached him about my plan to write a book about our team in which I would keep a journal throughout the season. He encouraged me the way I thought he would and, as stated in the Introduction, I soon started these journal entries.

One of the proudest moments of the summer for me occurred on a rainy Saturday morning when we had no scheduled workouts. Most of the players see this as a day off, but some of us viewed it as a day to get ahead of the rest of the SEC. On Saturday mornings Chris Lofton and I have been running what we call "stadiums" with our strength coach—Troy Wills. We go into Neyland Stadium and run from the bottom of the steps to the top concourse area. We do this 15 times while wearing a 25 pound weight vest. This weight vest looks much like a bulletproof vest.

If you are wondering how we get into Neyland Stadium, it's simple. We just walk straight in and act like we are supposed to be there. The first time we did this conditioning our legs were shaking and I was worried my legs were going to give out and I would fall down 55 rows of bleachers. It has not gotten much easier but our conditioning has improved.

This particular Saturday was a little different because it was raining. Jordan, who is always doing extra work, was going to run with us and called to see if we were still going. I told him I was pretty sure we were and to meet us at the stadium. I picked up Josh Tabb, who also was going to run with us. Josh has a cast on his hand and he isn't supposed to get it wet. I wasn't about to let him use a wet cast as an excuse not to run, so I searched my car and found an old Subway plastic sandwich bag, which he used to cover his cast. We get to the stadium and Jordan, Chris, Josh, and I are looking at each other in the pouring rain like "Are we really going to do this?" Troy shows up with the weight vests and we walk on in as if it was a beautiful day.

We begin running our "stadiums" in the rain, and it proved to be enjoyable. I liked it because there was no way anyone was working harder than us. Here we are in the pouring rain, running in silence and thinking to ourselves, "This is crazy." We finished up and everyone was exhausted and completely soaked. As we walked to our cars, soaking wet with the rain still coming down, I thought to myself, "What a beautiful sight."

I know it may sound weird but this is the kind of dedication it takes to become winners, and it is becoming contagious among our players. The dedication of our strength coach, Troy, can't be overstated. There can't be too many strength coaches who will do something like this to help players improve. He really pushes us in a way that makes us feel we have done all we can do. Who would have known that a rainy Saturday morning would come to be one of our defining moments of the preseason?

My days did a complete 180 and I can no longer brag about taking a nap after morning workouts, because I got a job. I wanted to do some type of work other than being a basketball camp counselor every summer. My dream is to continue playing basketball professionally, but I know the odds are against me and I need a backup work plan. Pete DeBusk, founder of DeRoyal, offered me the opportunity to serve a mini-internship with his company. My new summer schedule includes weights 7:45-9:30 a.m.; DeRoyal 10:30 a.m.-3:30 p.m. and workouts 4-5:30 p.m.

Within the limits of the short work day, the DeRoyal employees were great working with me to optimize the use of this time. I arrived at work at 10:30 a.m. and usually left for lunch within thirty minutes with a group of fellow employees. Five-hour days and lunch as soon as I get to work is something I could handle. We joked that I was the company's "lunch specialist." While at DeRoyal, I sat in on meetings, shadowed sales reps, and made "intern work" computer entries. The range and scope of DeRoyal's products and employment opportunities astonished me. It's amazing that Mr. DeBusk could start and grow his company to be so big and successful. For me, it was an interesting work experience. Now I will have something on my resume rather than being just a former UT athlete. I made several good friends at the company, and on my last day of work I told them as lunch specialist, "We'll do lunch sometime, just for old times sake."

Last year, Coach Pearl won a company golf tournament sponsored by DeRoyal. One day while I was working with Jack Payne, a super guy who organizes that golf tournament, he told me that Coach Pearl never got his trophy. Payne goes to a closet and asks me to deliver to Coach one of the biggest trophies you have ever seen. You would have thought Coach Pearl won the U.S. Open.

This was a good opportunity to pull a little joke on Coach Pearl. I covered up the plaque with some paper and wrote, "2006 SEC RUNNER-UP COACH OF THE YEAR." Last season Coach Pearl was picked Associated Press Coach of the Year, but John Brady was picked by the coaches. I attached a Post-it note that read, "Bruce - The SEC sent this to the wrong place. Hope you're having a good summer. Go Tigers! John Brady." Coach was out of town so I put it on his desk. When he returned, it wasn't difficult for him to identify the jokester. I heard through the grapevine that he was going to get me back by trying to fool me with eligibility issues. Soon, he asked me to call him about "something." So I returned his call and he tells me to check my e-mail because he received a letter from compliance saying I had some eligibility issues. I tried to play along at first, but couldn't help but laugh and told him I was a step ahead of him and to keep trying. He said, "I'll get you back as soon as I decide the starting lineup!" This shows that Coach has a great sense of humor, and can joke with a member of his basketball team while being a fearless leader of the team. A copy of my e-mail follows:

TO: Dane Bradshaw
FROM: Tyler Johnson
Assistant Athletics Director for Operations
DATE: July 31, 2006
RE: Eligibility for Fall 2006

The office of the University Registrar has contacted our office regarding your academic eligibility for the Fall 2006 semester. The Registrar has indicated that you are still missing one course for graduation and that your diploma was issued by mistake. An internal audit caught the mistake and a letter from the Dean's office in the College of Communications has acknowledged an advising error by your faculty advisor.

Please contact Coach Pearl as soon as possible regarding this information.

Lauren Mackey is out of town this week so I am trying to work with the Registrar's Office regarding this matter. Our Compliance Director may try to contact you soon, but please do not respond to his calls until you have spoken with Coach Pearl or myself.

Please contact me if you have any questions.

§§§

Toward the end of the summer session, I decided to "clear myself" to play for the first time since surgery. I wouldn't have done this if I felt like there was any chance of harm. It was so pleasing to hear my name as we picked teams, and just to be included was exciting. For months I had been off to the side doing something separate from the team. In the weight room, I would go off alone with one dumbbell and do single left-hand arm exercises, while the others partnered up to do bench presses. On the court, I would go off to a side goal and work on left handed moves while the others went through workouts or played pickup. These events of isolation began to wear on me because I wanted not only to get better myself, but to also improve play with my teammates.

For the first few minutes of pickup play, I was just happy to be out there. Then my competitiveness kicked in, and soon I became frustrated with my rustiness. I obviously couldn't shoot the way I wanted to. I was prepared for that; some might say I haven't shot well my entire life. It was my poor ball-handling and overall timing that I didn't expect to be off so much. I left the gym a little discouraged. But after we played a few more games, the timing and conditioning began to return and I felt more comfortable and confident with the wrist. At this point, the wrist still hurts but the significant difference is that now the wrist will continue to get better rather than worse. August 17 is the date for my next trip to Indianapolis to see Dr. Rettig, so I'm anxious to see what he will say.

On the last Saturday before we had a little vacation time, Troy and I had our final round of "stadiums." Saturday at 8 a.m., Troy, Josh and I walked in Neyland Stadium with our 25 pound weight vests. I never got used to the "stadiums." They just seemed a little less miserable each time. I never wanted to do the "stadiums," but would feel guilty if I didn't. I figure I have the rest of my life to sleep in on Saturday mornings, but my senior year isn't the time. I would rather look back on my college career and say I missed a few parties rather than say I wish I had worked harder. That way, if my senior year doesn't end in storybook fashion, it truly wasn't meant to be. And I will not have to ask myself, "Could I have done more?"

On that same Saturday, Jordan Howell and I were going to T-Rec, the campus rec center, and hit the pool. The pool was closed but Steven Pearl, the coach's son, called us and told us to come over to their new pool. So we went to the coach's house to lie around the beautifully designed pool area. Coach Pearl came home and we helped bring in some groceries and he hung out by the pool with us.

It's fun to see our coach as a family man. At one point he told his wife, "I have four kids and we have to pay a guy 10 dollars to pickup dog crap in the back yard!?" Coach Pearl has a great relationship with his players off the court; it doesn't matter if you are the leading scorer or the last person off the bench. When a player says, "I was chillin' at Coach Pearl's," we know it's not kissing up to the coach; it is being able to have your coach as a friend as well as your coach.

When Coach Pearl was at UWM and they played their Sweet 16 game, the game location was within driving distance of the Division II school in Southern Indiana, where earlier in his career he coached his team to a national championship. The gym for the Sweet 16 game was packed with former players, friends, and fans from the Southern Indiana area. Coach Pearl establishes life-long relationships with his players and they want the best for each other. There aren't many coaches who can be an outstanding coach and good friend to their players and coaching staff at the same time. But it makes things easier when the team and coaching staff have each other's backs and work so hard together to win.

The summer has come to an end and Coach seems to be pleased with the way things went, both academically and athletically. I believe it was a very productive summer and the dedication and focus seem to be intact. Everyone worked hard, but if I were to give out some "post summer" awards this is how it would go.

Hardest Working—Jordan Howell and Chris Lofton

I would like to include myself but my injury wouldn't allow me to work as hard as these two. If there is anyone out there who deserves success, it is Chris and Jordan. To be a hard worker, you have to do more than the required work. The required work can take a lot out of you, so it takes real dedication to continue to do extra. Jordan is very important to the team and would love to see his role and playing time increase. I am confident that he will be successful in whatever he does, because you can't find a harder or a better worker. I'm not sure if it will be a game-winning shot or earning a starting spot, but something positive has to be heading his way. Chris only knows hard work because hard work is what got him to where he is. He couldn't depend on athleticism, although he uses his deceptive quickness to his advantage, yet people continue to doubt parts of his game and he continues to prove them wrong. Sometimes when I get to the gym early, Chris will already be there at work. Both of these guys had incredibly productive summers and when it comes to the end of the game, I want to be on their team because I know they have earned it.

Most Improved—Ryan Childress

Ryan was a combination hardest working and most improved. He dedicated himself the way I would want all of my teammates to. His strength, conditioning, physique, quickness, and vertical jump have all improved tremendously. I think he will have a much greater impact than he did his freshman year.

Best Freshman—Wayne Chism

Josh Tabb was hurt and Ramar Smith was not cleared in time to attend summer school. It was between Duke, Marques, and Wayne. All were impressive in their own ways. But Wayne proved himself as an immediate impact player, and I predict he will be a guaranteed starter. It is good to have someone really push Major Wingate. At this time I think he is a little ahead of Major. However, Major should come out on top as best big man due to his experience. Marques is the sleeper and has the potential to be a pro with his height and vision at the guard position, but Wayne was the most impressive throughout the summer.

Starting Five Prediction

This is simply for entertainment purposes, and we will see how things actually pan out. Almost all of our players are good enough to start, but my guesses at this point are:

PG- Ramar Smith
G- Chris Lofton
G- Dane Bradshaw (got to show a little confidence)
PF- Wayne Chism
C- Major Wingate

JaJuan Smith will most likely find his way to the starting lineup, but I hope I'm in there somewhere.

August 21, First Team Meeting

Our first meeting as an entire team was held today with all the players reporting back to campus to kick off the new school year. There were plenty of topics to be covered, and we met for nearly an hour-and-a-half. Coach Pearl spoke about summer activities and how proud he was of our academics. We finished with a team grade point average of 3.1 for the summer, which is the best team GPA in years. Improvements are definitely being made. Coach continued to stress the importance of being responsible off the court to prevent team distractions. Also Coach told us they continue to bring in and build the basketball program around good people. This is a result of the incoming class being good representatives of the university and also our new assistant coach Steve Forbes.

There is a ton of paperwork that is required for NCAA compliance purposes at the beginning of each year. We have to register our cars and tell how and where we got them. We must describe any summer job we had and report the amount of money earned. We have to sign sheets saying we have not and will not participate in any sports-related gambling. All this is aimed at keeping our program free of any NCAA violations. The compliance efforts have to make sure that no one's eligibility is in jeopardy, which could have a direct effect on the team. Following some of the tedious compliance rules can be frustrating, but it is important to keep college athletics as clean as possible.

No matter what the situation, we can never accept extra benefits. This can be very hard because someone can recognize you as a player and offer you a free appetizer or something, but as an athlete that is considered an extra benefit and is an NCAA violation. The average person would be thrilled because everyone enjoys a free hookup, but we just can't do it. Compliance tells us that if what we receive is not offered to the entire public then we cannot accept it.

After we filled out forms, Coach addressed Ramar Smith's situation to the team. Ramar was not on campus and had yet to be cleared by the NCAA. This was due to a recent test score and academic eligibility questions. The staff has gone through a lot with Ramar and it is hard for him to sit at home waiting for the NCAA ruling so he can get on with his life. Ramar has made a passing test score but because his grades were sub-par before, the NCAA is questioning his eligibility. The more it drags on, the more classes he is going to miss. I don't see how he will play this year because it seems to be too late to get started. Coach recognized the fact that Ramar would have made us better, but he is confident in the talent we already have and believes we will have no problem being successful. This makes the point guard situation a little more interesting and I think it will be more of a point guard by committee in which a few players will rotate sharing the minutes. This is the spot I want and have always wanted, but we will have to see how things develop in the next couple of months.

August 22, Graduate School

Today was my orientation for graduate school. I will be working toward a Masters in Sport Management. I originally looked into the MBA program but was advised that it would be extremely tough to handle while playing. My schedule is about what I imagined for my senior year. All my classes are on Tuesday and Thursday. Being off Monday, Wednesday, and Friday allows me to get plenty of extra shots and extra work on my game while the other players are in class. I thought about taking an easy course like racquetball, but that didn't fly with my parents.

A sidebar of my early graduation last year is other players are envious and it motivates them to graduate. Most of them would prefer to have an easier schedule for their senior year, just as I did.

August 26, Start of Official Workouts

Official workouts begin on Monday, August 28, so Coach Pearl invited everyone out to his house for a cookout by the pool before things get really busy. We were supposed to be at his place by two o'clock, so I decided to try to get some shots up before going. In years past, I would have just gone by myself and been happy. But now I have a leadership role, so I called a bunch of my teammates and asked them to work out with me. This way the entire team is getting better. Hopefully, the rest of the SEC basketball teams are sleeping in.

We all went to Coach Pearl's home for the afternoon. I continue to be amazed at the closeness of the team and how comfortable the setting is between the coaching staff and the players. Overall, it was a great day at Coach's and nice to relax a bit before jumping into high gear on Monday.

Usually we have early morning weights on Monday but this semester we have quite a few players with 8 a.m. classes so we have weights in the afternoon. This is strange for me because I have no classes and haven't slept in on a Monday my entire life. So today I slept in and went to get some shots up around 10 a.m. Jordan Howell is done with his Monday class by then, so he and I worked on our shots together. Jordan and I have been workout partners since we stepped on campus.

After shooting, I went to a daily mass down the street from my apartment. I go to mass every Sunday, but there has been a lot on my mind lately and I just felt, today, the best place for me was church. The beginning of school is always a fun week, but it is full of temptations. There are numerous parties and it seems beautiful and approachable girls are everywhere I look. College is supposed to be one of the most fun times of an individual's life. Lately, I have begun to question myself on whether I should be taking more advantage of my position and participate in more parties and fun activities. My family, religion and dedication to basketball have kept me grounded in many ways, including issues of morality. However, now it seems more than ever, additional temptations confront me.

With basketball picking up, I start wondering more and more about my future. I know most college students have questions and fears about their future, when their college days start winding down. The same goes for an athlete.

It's hard to believe, after almost twenty years, I may be in my last year of organized basketball. I wonder if I will go into coaching or have an opportunity to play after college or if I will enter the world of business. With the campus environment and basketball expectations starting to weigh more on me, I felt a little extra time in church would help. The daily mass did help me put things in perspective and to be strong enough to look past my worries and perceived obstacles. I have always been taught, "To whom much is given, much is expected." The Lord has blessed me in many ways and I wish and hope to live in a Godly manner. By no means am I saying I am perfect and never go out and have fun. I enjoy partying, but I feel the Lord wants me to maintain a healthy balance between enjoying the fun times of college, yet staying dedicated and living the way He wants me too. I am very fortunate to have found my girlfriend, Julia, whose feelings for me do not vary with my worldly successes or failures. As far as my future goes, I was able to remind myself that the Lord has a plan for me and I should put my trust in Him. I should never doubt what path the Lord will lead me down. Obviously, a little extra prayer time helped me deal with my perceived problems and deeper questions about the mysteries and uncertainties of life.

August 29, Drug Testing Day & First Day of Individuals

Tuesdays are tough because we have 6:30 a.m. conditioning with Troy, but today we had to report by 6 a.m. for team drug testing. My alarm went off at 5:30 a.m. and I kept reminding myself not to pee, because if I did I would be stuck later drinking water so I could pee for the drug test. We all gave our urine samples. Then we went to the indoor football complex and began our conditioning. For the most part it was more speed mechanic drills and agility. Then when we thought we were done we heard the dreaded command, "300-yard shuttles." Three-hundred-yard shuttles have been a personal nightmare since I stepped foot on campus. They are absolutely miserable. We have two groups: the bigs and the guards. You have to sprint to the 10-yard line and back, 20-yard line and back..30..40..50 and back. This is in a dead sprint and the time to get back is usually about 55 seconds. It is both a conditioning drill and mental toughness drill. Fortunately, we only had one of them. But then we had a 150-yard shuttle followed by a 60-yard shuttle. We only did one of each today but we will increase them as the weeks go by. We finished at about 7:30 a.m. and I had to rush to the locker room to take a shower so I could make it to my 8 a.m. class.

Today was also the first day of individuals. Individuals are basketball practices with no more than four players at a time. The NCAA allows two hours per week in which a coach can work with the players, but only four players at a time. We break it up into a 45-minute individual on Tuesday and Thursday then a 30-minute individual on either Friday or Saturday. This equals the two-hour limit. My individual group consisted of Tony Passley, JaJuan Smith, and Steven Pearl. I switch groups, with each individual alternating between the wings and big men. These groups bothered me some because I wanted to compete for the starting point guard spot. Being put in groups with the wings and big men, makes it clear that our coaching staff is not looking at me as a possible point guard. I felt I had as much experience at the spot as anyone, and no one, to my knowledge, has clearly become a favorite at the position. Especially since Ramar Smith appears to not be eligible this year, I was hoping I would get a look. I didn't worry about it much because I have so much trust in our coaching staff that I know they will put each player in a position for the team to best succeed.

Individuals were really tough. No matter how well you condition yourself in the off season, you are never fully prepared for the first individual. The only reward of being in half-decent shape is you won't be quite as sore the next day. Assistant Coach Jason Shay usually is in charge of individuals, but this year new Assistant Coach Steve Forbes helped run things. Coach Forbes got after us from the start and made his presence felt early. We were doing a drill where we were supposed to sprint to the wing, set our feet properly, and shoot. "Sprint! Sprint!" Forbes yelled and I honestly thought we were going hard but he obviously didn't. He said, "Bring it in. You guys aren't sprintin'! This has to be game speed, come on!" So the message was clear and we went all out. After the drill was done and we were worn out with our hands on our shorts, Forbes says, "OK, that's how we are going to warm up each day." Warm up?! We thought we had gotten one of the harder drills out of the way first; little did we know we had just finished a warm-up drill. The individuals went on. We did some defensive close out drills and some two-on-two work. In the 2005-06 campaign, our team was last in the conference in defensive rebounding. A popular phrase in basketball is, "Defense and rebounding win championships." Since we were substandard in this area last season, you can tell it is a main focus this preseason. Coach Forbes established his "No B.S." reputation early.

Everyone got through the individuals and we are happy for the day to be over. It started at about 5:30 a.m. and ended around 4 p.m. Most of the guys also have to go to study hall and go to tutors around 7 p.m. I can't tell you how happy I am to not have to go to study hall; missing it makes your day so much easier. If we do well enough in the classroom, Coach rewards us with less study hall. If, on the other hand, a player doesn't do well, then he continues to serve many hours in the Thornton Center. The Thornton Center is a great resource. It is for athletes only and has a wonderful computer lab, a writing center and all the tutors you need to be successful in the classroom. We are fortunate to have it. But at the same time we try our best to do well in the classroom, so we don't have to spend so many hours in the Thornton Center study hall.

After a long day, it is interesting to see who shows the extra dedication to come to night shooting. Night shooting is an optional time from 9-10 p.m. to get up extra practice shots. Managers are there to rebound for us. We have the best managers in the country. If you think managers are just guys handing us water bottles and doing laundry, you're wrong. The managers, like the players, have time-consuming jobs. Coming to rebound at 9 p.m. is just one example of their dedication. We usually know which players will show up for night shooting. The guys you can count on seeing each night are Chris, Jordan, Tony, and me. Lately, Ryan Childress has been there consistently. Anything we can do extra will help the team, and night shooting falls into this category. We are fortunate to be in a program that provides so many opportunities to improve. I'm not sure there are many basketball programs in the country that require their managers to work at 9 p.m.

August 30, Ramar Smith is Eligible to Play

The big news for today is that Ramar Smith was cleared by the NCAA and will be eligible to play for us this year. This was incredibly good news for our team and bad news for the rest of the SEC. Ramar and the coaching staff have been through unbelievable trouble with the NCAA clearinghouse. To finally have success is very exciting. Coach Pearl told me the news in the weight room and said the team chemistry was so good right now that he did not want to make a huge deal over the announcement. He asked me as a senior to inform the guys and let them know the media would probably make a bigger deal out of it than he would.

I was interested to see the reaction of the guards when they learned that another high profile guard was coming in. Most of us have a team-first attitude, but it is human nature to want fewer people to compete with for any job. Everyone seemed fine with it and went about their business as usual. Jordan Howell is probably the player who feels most affected. He is an unbelievable person and one of the more unselfish players on the team. Jordan only wants the best for the team and will welcome Ramar with open arms, but, from a playing-time standpoint, it seems like things have gotten tougher. Jordan is religious and he and I are close, so I reminded him that the Lord has a plan and not to doubt what He has in store for him. Because of his faith, I think that thought helped him a little.

I got Ramar's cell phone number and decided to call and congratulate him. He answered and I told him who was calling and told him, "Thanks for screwing up everybody's minutes; you have really pissed off a lot of people around here. Playing time seemed guaranteed until your butt got cleared." Of course I was kidding and he laughed and you could tell in his voice what a relieved, excited person was on the phone. He found out in the afternoon and had to hop in the car and drive from Detroit to Knoxville. We had to get him here as soon as possible so he could start his class work.

August 31, A Tough First Week of Conditioning

We had our individuals and weights again today. Everyone's body is really starting to wear down after a tough first week. The freshmen especially are feeling the effects of major Division I workouts. In fact, Marques Johnson was so sore he told me not to say anything funny because it hurt him too bad to laugh. Coach Pearl is very good about recognizing and understanding the players' bodies and moods. So after individuals, Coach Pearl came to me and mentioned that we may take Monday (Labor Day) off, mainly for the freshmen because he doesn't want them to break down physically.

Because I am the senior player, Coach Pearl now has more communication with me. He lets me know ahead of time some of his decisions regarding the team. With that in mind, he told me to make the guys aware that if we kept working hard and no one screws up in the classroom that we would take Monday off. This is plenty of motivation for the team.

We were scheduled to have weights in the afternoon, but I was going to have to make them up on Friday due to my Thursday night class. I have some interesting classmates in this Thursday night class. Craig Pinkerton, our SID, is working on his master's and is taking the class. Also, Ken Johnson (KJ), Director of Basketball Operations, is sitting next to me in class. It is unusual when the assistant coach is comparing classroom notes with one of his basketball players. KJ does a lot of checking to make sure players are not skipping class, and I joke to my teammates saying, "You think it's bad KJ is checking your class, but he is actually *in* my class. There is no way I can cut that class."

My longest day of the week is over and I need to get to bed early for the big test of the week… THE HILL.

September 1, The Hill

Here we are 6:30 on Friday morning. This is one of our big conditioning/mental tests of the week. Also, it keeps everyone from going out on Thursday nights, which usually is a big student party night. We call it *The Hill* but it is actually Gate 10 of Neyland Stadium. Gate 10 is an entrance into the stadium that has a very steep incline, and most people are exhausted just by walking up it. Today, we have to run up it 11 times in 11 minutes. We sprint up and walk down, and obviously you don't want to take any longer than one minute going up and down to stay on pace. We will do this every Friday morning and increase three reps each week, eventually getting to 26 reps. I think the task is easier when you have all your teammates going through it with you. We got through it fine today and there were no vomit stories, but everyone was worn out. I had to go make up my weight lifting that I missed due to class the day before. I just wanted to get weights over with and lie on my couch the rest of the day because I don't have class on Fridays.

After being as lazy as possible all day, I decided to get up and do some extra night shooting. I knew I wouldn't go out tonight because of Saturday workouts, and I knew I was going out after tomorrow's football game. Here it is Friday night on the first football weekend and I, a 22-year-old college student, am heading to the gym to shoot basketballs. Before going to the gym, I decide to pickup a few items at the grocery store. I try to watch what I eat, and as I was checking out of the grocery store with my reduced fat Wheat Thins and no beer, it hit me. What a loser! I couldn't possibly be lamer. However, once I got in the gym I loved it. I was just going to get a few shots up, but once you get in the gym it becomes addictive. I ended up staying for more than an hour and was a sweaty mess, but it was the best my repaired wrist had felt, and I left that night with the most confidence I've had in my shooting for a long while.

September 2, Football Saturday

Saturday morning and the tailgating has already begun for the California game. Everyone around town has been saying that people are getting excited for basketball the same way they do football, but there is nothing compared to football time in Tennessee. We have individual workouts today and then play pickup from 1:30 to 2:30 p.m. These pickup games are open to the public. There was a sizeable crowd watching us, even though we don't publicize our Saturday workouts in the media. I think more and more will come each Saturday. It's a nice break from the heat at the tailgates for the fans. I thought we played well, Wayne especially. I think we made the fans even more excited about our upcoming season.

After playing pickup, there were burgers and brats waiting for us in the parking lot where the coaches and their families were tailgating. I love going to the games, but they end up wearing us out on Saturday morning. Then the last thing I want to do is stand in the student section for three hours. But I sucked it up and went to the game. Coach, Chris, and I had a little promo on the Jumbotron during the game. It was fun to hear the applause of the football fans as they showed their anticipation for basketball season. This Volunteer fan reaction is new for me after going through some disappointing years. The media has done an excellent job of helping keep the excitement of basketball year round. However, with basketball news in the newspaper for the third straight day, Coach thought it was taking away from football. He certainly didn't want it to seem as if basketball was trying to upstage or compete against football for media attention. I'm not sure anyone else viewed it this way, but he did.

The football team put any speculation about media competition to rest with a convincing win and everyone was happy for them. Football is King in Tennessee. Coach Phillip Fulmer and the football team came through huge—the way they consistently seem to do as soon as people start doubting. We are around the football players and coaches so often that we cheer, not only as fans but as caring friends. So we were all pleased to see a great start to the season.

Tonight was my night to enjoy myself as a college student and get out with some friends. Every place we went was packed with proud Vol fans celebrating the victory over California. Like all college students, I definitely enjoy 'letting loose' on the weekends. Yet, I know that I need to party more responsibly than the average student because my actions reflect on myself, my teammates, my coaches and the program.

September 4, Labor Day

Coach gave us Labor Day off and everyone was happy and excited about that. If we wanted to get up shots, the gym was opened from noon to 3 p.m. I expected to see the normal players I see at night shooting, but was pleasantly surprised to see almost the entire team there to participate in a nonmandatory work out. That is the type of team dedication we need and I left the gym very proud to be part of the team.

September 5, Back to the Grind

At 6:30 a.m. we returned to our conditioning and it was harder than ever, but there was nothing that happened today more critical than the news of Major Wingate. Major had been reinstated to the team. But after serving a long suspension, he was in a "no tolerance" situation. One more screw-up and he is gone. I got a text message from Major during the day that read, "I need to talk to you." This was abnormal and I surmised something was wrong. I expected a worst-case scenario. He didn't answer my call, but I knew I would soon see him in the locker room for pickup. As the other players went on to the gym floor, Major and I stayed in the locker room and talked. I could tell it was serious and he said, "I'm kicked off the team." I put my head down in disappointment. As Major explained himself in an innocent, emotional way I had mixed emotions. I have been with Major for more than three years, and it was tough to see my friend with tears in his eyes. I felt for him, but I may have been more upset than sympathetic. Everyone loved Major, but his actions put our season in jeopardy. Major left me with a ray of hope when he said he was going to meet with Mike Hamilton, Athletic Director, and do his best to convince Mr. Hamilton to let him stay on the team.

Almost stunned, I went out to play pickup. Before we started playing, Coach Pearl called me to the side and asked if I knew anything about Major's situation. JaJuan and I were the only ones that Major had told, but JaJuan had told Chris, so Coach felt like it was necessary to hold a team meeting. He called everyone into the locker room. Most of the players had no idea what we were meeting about. Coach started off by saying, "There is a 99 percent chance that Major is kicked off the team…let that sit for a minute." He then said that it was basically out of his hands and that the situation was in Mike Hamilton's hands. Pearl felt like Major had been given more than enough chances and had been surrounded with the necessary resources to change and succeed, but he just wouldn't. Coach still feels like, on some level, he failed Major as a coach and a friend. I believe we did all we could do, but one always wonders if they could have done more. Coach continued to stay confident in the talent we had and told us that we will just have to wait and see what happens.

Coach Pearl called me later in the night to talk about Major. He was going to put up a fight for Major, but said he could only go so far in good conscience, because he believed he didn't deserve another chance. Coach said he felt for me as a senior going through this. He says to the seniors, "This is your team, not mine. I'm going to be part of plenty more teams, but this is your last team." Major was scheduled to meet with Mr. Hamilton in the morning and Coach didn't feel very confident as he got off the phone.

September 6, Major Wingate is Dismissed from the Team

I got an early morning call from Assistant Coach Jason Shay, telling me that Major had officially been kicked off the team.

The news would be released to the media today. It is hard to explain my emotions because I felt so bad for Major. On the other hand, it was hard for me to sympathize too much because he had been warned time and time again. The fault was his own, and because of his actions our whole team suffered. Wayne is going to do great things, but he would have flourished at the power forward position alongside Major. But now Wayne is our only potential center at 6'8". Duke is a possibility too, yet he is also undersized. For me personally, my hopes of playing some point guard are gone. Like last year, I'm stuck at the emergency power forward position. I am willing to do all I can for the team, and this gives me more opportunities to play. But here in my senior year when all the pieces seemed to fit, all of a sudden, the team now has a 6'8" undersized freshman center and a 6'3" undersized guy at power forward. I know we will get through it and UT isn't the only team that has personnel problems. We will have to see how the team responds and Bruce Pearl will have to demonstrate why he gets the big bucks, again.

September 7, More on Major Wingate

Major's dismissal was announced as a violation of team rules, but the media, citing their sources, reported it as a failed drug test. Major was ranked the number one eighth grader in the country. He was ranked above LeBron James and looked like a sure NBA draft pick right out of high school. At a young age, he had a lot of expectations and pressures thrown at him, and I believe these had a direct impact on his later behavior.

I know Major is not a bad person. I truly believe he is a good person at heart. He just has some self-discipline problems. The public perception shouldn't be that he is a bad guy. I hate that he can't be alongside me to experience the special times of a senior season. I plan to try and stay in touch with Major for the rest of my life. His mother is one of the sweetest ladies in the world and Major has that same sweetness in his heart. You could see that in the way Major would interact with the community. He would go out his way to be nice to fans or do something special for a child who looked up to him. He put in a lot of work at the Boys and Girls Club and touched many lives in a positive way. That was a side of Major that few people got to see. Hopefully, he will stay in school and stay in good academic standing. Coach Pearl will continue to try to help Major, specifically trying to get him into some overseas basketball league. We will be here for Major and wish him the best.

All the attention has focused on Major's situation but the players have responded well. The freshmen are going to have to grow up a little faster than planned, but we will be fine. Everyone has been working extremely hard despite the distractions of the past couple of days. I haven't even had a chance to talk about Ramar's play. I am anxious to see him in real game situations because he shows so much potential. He can dunk any way you want it, he can defend, he can knock down the open shot, he can pass, and he can push it up the court. I was waiting to see a flaw, but I haven't seen one. Jordan's experience and improved game will provide an interesting battle to keep an eye on at the point guard position over the next month or so.

I am heading to bed dreading tomorrow. We have 14 trips up and down Gate 10 at 6:30 a.m. I remind myself how lucky I am to be in this position and that I need to appreciate every day of it.

September 8, Back to the Hill

Gate 10 actually was not too bad. The weather is getting cooler, which helps. I went to my locker and everyone had the same thing posted up on the inside of their locker. It was a list of successful teams that had managed to win despite the lack of size.

Illinois went to the national championship in 2005 and Villanova went to the Elite 8 in 2006; both teams started four guards. This was an effort to keep our goals set high despite losing our big man—Major. Major came by the gym today during individuals and everyone was very supportive and courteous. I talked to him and said, "You know I feel for you, but I'm pissed at you too." He said, "I know, I know." We had a casual conversation and he left with our friendship intact, which made me feel better about the situation.

I made some progress today in trying to put this book together. I spoke with compliance before making any type of contractual agreements, because I was not sure if I would be breaking NCAA rules. I was informed that while a player has eligibility remaining they cannot have any contract agreements for a publication concerning the season, even if it is to be published after their eligibility is finished. In other words, I can contact people about aspects of publishing the book but can't make any official agreements until after the season. Also, I wanted to contact Jerod Haase. Jerod is a former Kansas Jayhawk player who was successful in writing a book about his senior year, similar to what I'm trying to do. I don't know the first thing about publishing a book and perhaps Jerod could provide me some helpful advice. I found he is now the Director of Basketball Operations at North Carolina and Craig Pinkerton got me his contact information. I'll try to call Jerod Monday, but I am excited about the fact that my book idea has a chance.

September 10, NFL Opening Sunday

There are no commitments for me today, and I plan to watch NFL football. It is opening Sunday and this is my favorite sport to watch. I am a lifelong Philadelphia Eagles fan. This may sound strange, since I am from Memphis. But as a kid I loved to watch Randall Cunningham play. I could go on and on about being a fanatic fan, but I'll just let a game ritual of mine suffice. Among many jerseys I have purchased are a Donovan McNabb jersey (quarterback) and a Brian Dawkins jersey (safety). Thus, I have an offense and defense jersey. I find it necessary to switch my jerseys as the Eagles go on offense and defense. It's just something I do as a loyal fan, which also makes some friends laugh. Of course, I only do this when I am watching the game at home.

Once in a while I am asked to speak at a camp, church, birthday party, etc. Tonight I was asked to speak to an eighth grade etiquette class on sports etiquette in basketball. I was happy to do it, but laughed because I should probably be the one taking the class. My language is at its worst when I play, and I grew up playing in some rough parts of Memphis where etiquette was the last thing on players' minds. As a result, I find the thought of me talking to anyone about etiquette a little humorous. Fortunately, I was able to pull my sports etiquette speech off and perhaps the kids learned something. Eighth graders with blank stares and disinterested looks can be a tough crowd to reach. I know because that was me not too many years ago, and I don't envy teachers trying to drag class participation from a group of bored eighth graders.

September 11, Team Individuals

It is Monday morning and I get a text message that reads, "The next person to miss or be late to class, tutor appointments, study hall, or workouts the whole team will run at 6 a.m." I was upset with this because we are too early into the semester to be getting this kind of threat, and the reality is that someone will be late for something sooner or later.

This week is supposed to be a week for everyone to get their legs back and rest. The reason is we officially are allowed to start team individuals on Friday. This means that our whole team can be on the court in a real practice-type setting, rather than four players at a time as we have been doing. Coach Pearl has designated times for us to get shots up this week rather than having individuals. Needless to say everyone was glad, because getting shots up with a manager is a lot easier than individual workouts with the coaches. It looks like the hardest part of the week will be tomorrow morning's conditioning and Gate 10, which was moved to Thursday morning so we could be fresh for Friday's practice.

September 12, Not One of Our Better Days

This is not a good day. We have 6:30 a.m. conditioning and a few people are missing. Great. They just warned us that the whole team will have to run for the next person that is late, and in less than 24 hours we have guys screwing up. We went ahead and started. The guys who were late jumped in the workout as they got there. We ended the conditioning with the dreaded 300-yard shuttles. We are all exhausted and glad to have conditioning over. Then KJ and Coach Shay huddle us up. They told us they had warned us, but we clearly didn't get the message so we will have to meet at 6 a.m. tomorrow for a team run. This is bad news to hear when you are already dead from running sprints. KJ told us the coaching staff will give us some slack and understands that "sh#@ happens," but it is happening too often and because of that we will run until we get the point. Shay felt like we were taking our basketball opportunity for granted and referred to Inky Johnson on the football team. Inky went down with an injury last Saturday against Air Force and may never be able to play again. Shay told us that we can never know what the future brings, and that we better start putting everything into each day. We all left for class in sour moods and went about our day, but I know most of us are thinking about what is in store for us tomorrow morning.

September 13, Group Punishment

It's raining; it's supposed to be my day to sleep in and I'm walking to my car at 5:30 a.m. to go run for something that wasn't my fault. So I'm more than a little pissed off. I get to the football complex where we are running on the indoor field and the weight vests are waiting on us. Wonderful, not only do we have to run but we have to run with an extra 25 pounds strapped to us. We start off with defensive slides, which burns your legs. I started to think this is all we were going to do, which wouldn't be too bad. Wrong! I could not have made a more inaccurate assumption. Shay splits us up in two groups; guards and posts. We are to start at the back of the end zone and run a suicide the length of the field. What this means is that we have to touch each line in 10-yard increments and come back to the starting point until we have touched the other goal line. So here it is, much like a 300-yard shuttle but way longer. Start at the back of the end zone, touch the goal line and come back, touch the 10-yard line and come back, touch 20 and come back, 30, 40, 50, then the other 40, 30, 20 10, goal line, and ends at the opposite end zone. I calculated this while I was running and it was a 1,440 yard shuttle with a weight vest. It took about six minutes and some people were hurting.

After the other group was finished, we were told to get back on the line and that if we didn't finish in six minutes we would do it again. As I finished my run, I knew I had made my time but there were a couple of guys who definitely were not going to make it. One of those guys was the main reason that we were running, so I was very upset. When this particular player asked me if we were done, I said, "I don't know; you didn't make your damn time." That set off an argument between us in which I pointed out that we were running for him already and he was going to end up making us run again for him, because he couldn't make his time since he was not trying hard enough. The argument got louder and louder, but I didn't care. I felt I needed to step up and say something. The team not taking care of their business is a reflection on me, as Team Captain, and shows a lack of leadership, so I had some strong words. It definitely wasn't good for two teammates to curse each other out. Eventually, Coach Shay intervened and actually seemed happy to see us getting on one another. The message was clear and we all left very pissed off, especially me. To top things off, I came out to my car to a 7 a.m. $32.00 parking ticket.

I worried about the altercation throughout the day because I didn't want an enemy on the team and was not sure I handled the situation in the best way. Also, I didn't want it to become a locker room issue where players were choosing sides. I'm the only senior with a lot of young freshman. We have players from many different backgrounds and it isn't easy for all of them to accept someone as a leader. I don't want to be called a leader and captain just because I'm a senior. I can't expect these guys to come in and just surrender to orders from some guy who happens to be a senior. I try to develop friendships first because it is easier to listen to a friend rather than someone just ordering you to do something. The last thing we needed was team dissension, but I felt like I had done the right thing. It reassured me when several players who witnessed the argument told me I was in the right and they were glad to see someone speak out.

September 14, Order is Restored

It was 6:30 a.m. at Gate 10 and Coach Pearl was back in town to restore order. After hearing that people had been late, he had some words for us. He gets his message across without being a jerk. He spoke to us in an intense, raised voice about how we don't have these workouts and run the hill as punishment, but rather to get better. He was tired of seeing people act like it was such a pain in the ass to work out and asked a rhetorical question, "How good did it feel to win last year and how bad did it suck to lose? So is it really worth it to put in the required work to win? I think it is!" Things like running Gate 10 at 6:30 a.m. are what make us champions and deserve victory. For the second time in as many days, a football player was used as an example for motivation. Coach Pearl spoke on Justin Harrill's highly publicized return for the Florida game despite a season ending injury with a torn biceps. That toughness and appreciation of the game are what Coach wanted us to show. Coach obviously knew about my altercation, because without using specific names he told us to be good receivers of criticism and accept leadership. He said that we may not like what is always being said, but we have to leave any arguments on the court or practice field. Coach's words helped quash any harsh feelings that may have carried over between me and my teammate. We began our run, and a simple high-five between me and the other player was enough for us to realize we were back on the same page; sometimes that can be enough and can take the place of "I'm sorry."

September 15, Start of Team Individuals

Today was our first team individual and there were definitely some areas that need work, although overall it was not too bad for the first team practice. With so many freshmen, the coaching staff understands that a lot of patience will be required. It takes time to adjust and there are some complicated things to learn. The upperclassmen realize this and we jokingly say we love it because we get a longer break in between drills to catch our breath. This is because Coach has to take more time to explain what he wants us to do. For me personally I missed a few open shots, which frustrates me, considering the time I spend putting up shots. I tried to remain positive for tomorrow's team individual.

September 16, An Exciting Football Saturday

It's a great day to be in Knoxville, Tennessee. The UT Vols football team plays the Florida Gators! Honestly, the basketball team couldn't wait to get practice over so that we could do some tailgating in preparation for the Vols football game that night. We didn't practice too hard because Coach took this day to focus on teaching some of the offensive sets. Many of the tailgaters came to the gym to get a glimpse of us, and it was fun to see the impact Coach Pearl had on these fans. While he explained the offense, the interested fans sat on the edge of their seats as if they were preparing for a game.

During practice I didn't make a shot and I wanted to just go lock myself in my apartment. I feel like I put as much work as possible into my shooting and during the first two days of practice I can barely make a shot. I shoot it well enough while practicing on my own; then I come to practice and throw up bricks. I am the first person to encourage a teammate who misses 10 shots in a row by saying, "Don't worry, keep shooting." If I had this same mind-set for myself, I would be better off. I don't believe my mind gets in the way while I'm shooting, but it really frustrates me that my hard work doesn't translate into better shooting percentages. It's especially frustrating, when I watch some of my teammates, who I know for a fact haven't put the time in the gym that I have, making more shots than me. I trust that my hard work will pay off in the end and that I will get better, but it was really tough on me today and I was really down.

Chris Lofton and I had to help present Coach Pearl as National Coach of the Year during a timeout in the football game. If it weren't for that I probably wouldn't have gone to the game, because I was so upset about my personal basketball progress. However, after practice, we had a big team tailgate party outside the arena. Tim Reese is the captain of our tailgates and is the man on the grill. The good food and festivities, plus being around the guys, cheered me up.

During the first timeout of the football game, Chris and I presented Coach Pearl, who was announced as the National Basketball Coach of the Year. One hundred thousand fans chanted "BRUUUCCCEEE!" and the Florida fans couldn't do a thing because if they booed it would just sound like they were joining in with the "BRUUCCEE" chant. I could tell Coach was getting emotional, and who could blame him. With his humble beginnings and now more than 100,000 people chanting his name, it was amazing. The rest of the team waited on the sidelines and when we returned there, the team jumped all over him as if we were getting hyped for a big game. It was also cool for me to walk out and hear the applause from fans when my name was mentioned. What a difference a year can make!

A bunch of the players and I went out on The Strip after the tough football loss. I was surprised at how many Florida faithful were in the bars. I guess most of the UT fans were upset with the loss and went home. I was even more surprised that a number of the Florida fans recognized me as the guy who made a game winning shot against their basketball team. At one club, my teammates and I were in the midst of some Florida fans and we were having fun trash talking one another. A couple of the Florida fans were at the end of the bar, and I asked the bartender to send them drinks on me. When they looked up to see who had sent the drink, I held a glass up and toasted, "Here's to us kicking your ass for the third straight time!" The look on their face was priceless and they immediately started laughing. I know it is a sin around Knoxville, but we actually had a good time with some of the enemy's fans. No need to worry; we still hate them.

September 18, Visit with Dr. Rettig

I had to make a five-hour drive to Indianapolis to see my wrist doctor, Dr. Rettig, hopefully for the last time.

Today I was officially cleared to play after six months of surgeries, several casts, and countless hours of rehab. When a top wrist doctor in the country clears me to play and says my wrist will continue to get better, it gives me extra confidence and assurance. I know it still hurts a little, but trust that it will get better. He told me I could start shooting without my wrist brace, but suggested that I continue to wear it during contact situations in practice. I traded a 10-hour round trip for a 10-minute checkup, but it was worth it. Dr. Rettig has been more than impressive with his extraordinary skills. After every checkup, he calls my home and reports to my mother because he knows how much concern she has about my health.

Fortunately, I have no classes on Monday and all I had to miss was a weight session. We are not having any individual workouts this week so that we can save our allowed two hours as a team for a good, hard practice with the coaches on Friday.

September 19, Horses#*@

I shot without a wrist brace today. It was strange because I have had something, whether it was tape, brace, cast, or a combination of things, on my wrist since the injury occurred on January 21. It felt really good as I shot, but I iced it right after to avoid soreness.

My dad called me to see how I was doing and shared yet another Coach Pearl story. Coach was in Memphis recruiting and a television reporter was digging at him and obviously trying to stir up controversy. The questions went something like, "How do you feel to be the number two team in the state? How are you going to get better than the University of Memphis team?" Coach Pearl continued to answer the questions politely and professionally. Finally, when the reporter threw another curve ball at him, Coach responded, "You wanna know what I really think? I think it's a horses#*@ question."

This wasn't highly publicized but we laughed that only Coach Pearl can say "horses#*@" on TV and gain fans.

September 20, Self-Pity

I was pretty upset with myself today because I let my emotions get the best of me. We played pickup this afternoon and I continued to struggle with my shot, but what really pissed me off was that my wrist was still so sore. After six months, I just mentally wasn't ready for another wrist hurdle. While playing basketball sometimes you get stuck on a team with guys that are only looking for their own shot at all times. That was my situation today. I was on a team that rarely passed and when I did shoot my hand hurt and I missed. A combination of things had me frustrated but it was mainly my shot and my wrist. I'm just tired of having pain in my wrist and just want to be able to play to my full ability, which I haven't been able to do for about nine months. Basically, I was whining, having a self-pity party and behaving like a baby. After I finished pouting, I was able to come back to reality and realize how fortunate I am. I know my problems are pittances compared to many, many other folks who must deal with significantly worse problems than I face.

September 21, Appreciate It & Picture Day

The alarm rings at 6 a.m. and I would give anything to stay in bed. The last thing I want to do is run Gate 10, but I have brainwashed myself that when my alarm goes off for situations like these to tell myself, "Appreciate it." I remind myself that this is the opportunity I have worked for and have wanted my whole life and soon it will be over, so I need to appreciate every aspect of being a student-athlete. By saying, "Appreciate it," I pop right out of bed and my complaining ceases. However, today I'm not sure many people would want to trade what they are doing with what I will be doing. It is cold, cold outside and we have to run 18 times up and down Gate 10.

We take off running and it is discouraging when you get to the top and say "One!" knowing you have seventeen more to go. It wasn't long before my nose was running and by about the seventh rep I couldn't help but feel a similarity between myself and Jim Carey in *Dumb and Dumber* as he drives to Aspen on a little scooter with snot disgustingly dried under his nostrils. This made me laugh for a second, but joy doesn't last long in this situation. I did finish without as much trouble as I normally have, and it was nice to see that my conditioning is improving. Marques Johnson and Jordan Howell continue to lead the group, not only because they are good natural runners, but because they are dedicated, hard workers.

Coach Pearl was out of town today and he tells us how much he hates being away. He reminds us that when we don't see him, he is working. We know that as we are running this morning that he is not just sleeping in somewhere. And, for some strange reason this is comforting to know. If Coach could be here, he would be, and he usually is.

We are excited about this afternoon because we have team pictures and have to film some things for the Jumbotron in the stadium. A real bonus is this activity will take the place of weights for the day. The setup was well thought out and looked extremely cool. There is a huge backdrop with a nice shade of blue, but the neatest part was the fog machines. They were able to spray some mist on the court and it looked like we were standing in the fog. It was awesome. Everyone always jokes with each other as we take our individual photos because we have to give a tough-guy look at the camera. Chris and I had some pictures together for what I think is the cover of the media guide. I told Chris he had better make it to the NBA so this can be more impressive for me. The players had fun with the added attention, joking with each other and looking forward to seeing the results of the promotions and the pictures.

September 22, Our First Controlled Scrimmage

We had our two-hour team individual today, which was a shortened practice. We continued to go over our offense, and for the first time we scrimmaged in a controlled setting. When I say controlled setting, I mean not just playing "pickup," but actually playing the game with offensive sets and playing with some coaching. I was on the team with Jordan, Chris, Tony, and Duke. We killed Ramar, Wayne, JaJuan, Ryan, and Marques. The main factor was strictly experience and familiarity with our system. Our team knew how to run the offense more effectively due to more experience. I wonder how this will play out into the season. I know everyone will continue to learn what Coach wants, but with so much competition for starting spots, I'm anxious to see if experience becomes a deciding factor. Only time will tell.

September 29, A Couple of Days Off

Everyone has been waiting anxiously for this Friday to come. This sounds strange considering we have to run Gate 10 twenty-two times today, but since the football team has the away game in Memphis, Coach Pearl decided to give us the weekend off. He wants to give us a chance to go home for the weekend or just relax and rest our bodies.

About a month back, I had asked Coach for permission to leave town this weekend, because one of my older brothers was getting married in Memphis. He felt this was a good opportunity to let everyone take a couple days to themselves. You can believe we were all in favor of this decision. I ran the dreaded Gate 10 and hit the road to my hometown of Memphis. A five-and-a-half hour drive was not the first thing I wanted to do after running Gate 10, but I couldn't wait to get home to see my family.

October 1, Cody and Vicky's Wedding

The rehearsal dinner, the wedding, and the reception were great fun. And they brought together family and friends. We got to catch up on a lot of past activities, so I'm worn out from the weekend.

I'm sure some may wonder who would plan a wedding in Memphis on the Saturday of a UT versus Memphis football game? Well, my brother, Cody, married a beautiful girl, Vicky, who is originally from Korea and this was one of the few dates her family could fly in from Seoul, South Korea.

Because of this situation, my mom, who did much of the wedding planning, couldn't tell people in Korea that we needed to switch the wedding date because of a football game. The wedding was at 7 p.m. Mother had hoped the game would be played during the day. Two weeks ago, when they announced the game time as 11 a.m., it was perfect. Our friends and family were now happy because they could attend the wedding functions without interfering with the big game.

The weekend was eventful for all of us, but especially so for my parents. It's difficult to entertain and communicate with a family that, for the most part, does not speak English. Vicky's family is very kind and sweet, so that made things a lot easier. To help with the language barriers, there was a translator at the wedding. Some of Vicky's family were courageous enough to give speeches at the rehearsal dinner.

During the reception, my mother's friend came to her and said, "I think you have a wedding crasher. There is a guy in shorts and an orange T-shirt." The wedding crasher turned out to be my Assistant Coach Forbes. He was in town for the game and I had invited him to come to the reception. When he called, he told me he only had shorts on. Since we were already deep into the reception, I told him to come on anyway, that no one was going to care. We had a blast and I was glad Coach Forbes met my family. We joked that I was trying my best to increase my playing time by bringing a coach to a family wedding. It was hilarious that Coach Forbes was labeled a wedding crasher.

In April we have a family trip to Korea for a "second wedding." My family is calling it the "Griswold's Korean Vacation." Yours truly will be fitted for a kimono for the second wedding. Yes, I will be in Korea after the season in my kimono. Perhaps I can get that picture posted on the UT sports website for somebody's merriment.

I realize that most readers didn't buy this book to read about my brother's wedding. But, behind the scenes, collegiate athletes have personal lives that are important long before and after their playing days.

October 2, No Night Shooting for Me

Speaking of personal lives, I had to get my night shooting out of the way during the day. Because tonight, I am celebrating our two-year anniversary with my girlfriend—Julia Taylor. Through high school, I never had a steady girlfriend and I was the guy who said I would never be locked down with one girl. This is why it's crazy that I have been in a relationship for two years with Julia, but I've got it good. Julia is a year behind me in school. We started dating in the midst of a 14-win/17-loss season, and the only reason she cares about the outcome of a game is its effect on me.

Being associated with an athlete is not on Julia's priority list. In fact, at games she prefers to go unnoticed, so she does not look like some sports groupie.

Julia and her family have taken me in, and it has been easier to make Knoxville home while I'm here because of them. I have the greatest parents in the world but they can't always be here. Don and Carol Taylor have been tremendous supporters, and I am blessed to have such a loving family here in Knoxville. I'm good friends with their oldest daughter, Libby, and treat their youngest daughter, Maria, like a little sister.

Anyway, I had to do the sweet boyfriend thing tonight with presents and dinner. Of course, as an athlete this means you hope workouts don't go over the usual time, sprint to the shower, write a card at the last minute and act like you're not completely too exhausted to go on a date. So, we went to our favorite restaurant in the Old City, Pasta Trio. Their salad and bread are incredible and I always order the filet stuffed with bleu cheese. We walked back to my apartment to exchange presents and cards to finish off my attempt at being a romantic boyfriend. If I'm starting to make some guys out there ashamed, don't worry. I strategically planned all this a little early to get this sweet stuff out of the way, because my Philadelphia Eagles have a big game and I have to get focused for Monday Night Football at 8:30. Fly Eagles Fly!

October 3, Coach Pearl's Meeting

We were going to have our normal Tuesday morning conditioning at 6:30, but we were told to get there by 6:15 so Coach Pearl could meet with us. This is never good and I was prepared to be chewed out. He started addressing some small issues with guys maybe not communicating well with their tutors or bad test grades. There was not one big issue, but he could tell some of us were starting to slack off and he needed to make us realize that these little problems can lead to bigger issues. We needed to head off problems before they developed. Another thing he addressed was a recent article featuring Duke Crews. Duke is from New Jersey and every player I have played with from the Northern area has a little extra swagger to them. It's not necessarily bad; it's just their culture of basketball. Duke had some quotes in the paper that were a little too confident. He proclaimed the freshman class as the "Fab Five" and said he is not sure who can beat us. Coach was glad to see the confidence, but knew it could be taken wrong by certain readers. He said, "Other teams may put this on their bulletin board but I don't really give a damn what other teams think. It's the community and the students I care about. They read this and think the basketball team has one good season and becomes cocky and arrogant. Be humble in everything you do." It's hard to convey the impact of Coach Pearl's message with mere words, because a significant part of his communication is the passion and intensity with which he speaks.

Another interesting point he made was on how everyone is trying to evaluate the freshmen. "Everyone wants to evaluate the freshmen, but there is nothing to evaluate yet. They haven't had a chance to do anything. What we should do is evaluate the class after their careers, not before. Evaluate how many championships or how many graduated! Not evaluate what we hope they will do!" Last, he got back to the fact that some of us need to refocus. This is when faces started turning red. He cited as an example the once-in-a-lifetime opportunity we will have to play in Madison Square Garden in the Preseason NIT, if we can win two games—one against Fordham and the winner of UNC-Wilmington versus Belmont. Obviously, this is a situation where we should win these two and head to MSG. He yelled, "How bad do you want it?! Is it worth it to cut corners for the feeling of losing and watching others play for your championship? Is it worth it?" He stressed that we need to address these problems now and learn our lesson now rather than having to learn from a tough loss to a team we should beat. Coach Pearl doesn't want us to wait to be given a wake-up call through a loss, but to wake up now.

October 6, My Last Gate 10 & Jordan's Injury

For me, today is a momentous day—the last Gate 10 of my life! Only 26 times, up and down Gate 10; I'll never have to do it again. If you don't know what Gate 10 is, please look for it as you head to the next UT football game, so we players can have a little of your sympathy.

This is it for me; suck it up for about 25 minutes and that will be it. I'm the only one who can say this is their last time since I'm the lone senior. I was challenged a few weeks ago when I heard that the seniors at the University-Wisconsin Milwaukee (the coaching staff's former school) would do something special, like run in nothing but their tights for the last run of their hill. I decided, also, to be creative for my last run but told none of my teammates about my plan.

As we run, we have people who are in the lead and then those that are a little behind, but we all wait and run the last rep together. I was one of the first to finish, so I had time to rest before everyone got down to run the last rep together. As we all began to gather at the bottom, I was ready for my grand finale for my last sprint up Gate 10. With the coaches, managers, strength coach and trainer standing at the bottom behind us, I rolled my shorts and tights down revealing my beautiful white ass for all to see. On this scroll I had written, "GO VOLS!"; "GO" on the left cheek and "VOLS!" on the right. I got some really loud laughs and took off in a dead sprint with my ass hanging out and "GO VOLS!" becoming smaller as I sprinted off into the distance. If nothing else, at least the coaching staff will have to remember me for my exclamation point about Gate 10.

Having finished my last hill run and with nothing else to do for the day, I was having a great day. Meanwhile Jordan was having a bad day. He had injured his wrist in a light, short practice yesterday in which Coach Forbes was going to lead us through some defensive drills while the rest of the coaches were out of town. Jordan was fighting through a screen when his right wrist was bent backwards. You could tell he was hurt bad right away. But being the tough guy, when asked if he needed to sit out the drill, he replied, "It's numb, but I'll be all right. Let's go." Most people would have gone to see the trainer right away, but you have to drag Jordan off the court.

X-rays today showed there was a break in the third metatarsal along with some other damage. His shooting hand was put in a cast, and he was told he had to be in it for a couple weeks, then a brace for another couple weeks. Hopefully, he will be playing in a month, which is in time for the first game. One might think, "It's just a month, not too bad." This is not the case with Jordan. Every year he has gotten a tough injury to overcome in the preseason and has to play catchup at the worst time. I hate it for him because he was playing the best he has played since coming here. He was healthy and battling hard for the starting spot at the point.

Jordan does not deserve a setback. He works extremely hard and disciplines himself on and off the court. Jordan was down today, and who can blame him. Obviously, I can relate to his situation and told him that going through some struggles before being rewarded is going to make it all the sweeter when he gets the big payoff. There is not much anyone can say to help Jordan's depressed feelings, but I believe something will happen in his last two seasons that will reward Jordan for his hard work, dedication, and willingness to fight through adversity.

October 10, Media Day

Today was official Media Day, an event where several reporters from local news channels and sports writers from around the area come around to speak with the players and coaches. Yesterday, we had some media training with Bob Kesling, the Voice of the Vols. With so many young players, the media attention can be overwhelming and all it takes is one verbal slipup to create a mess. We learned obvious things such as: don't guarantee anything, be humble, cooperate with the media, and be respectful of your opponents. In addition, we did mock interviews where we tried to eliminate "you know what I'm saying" and "Uh, um" from our vocabularies. Chris was the guinea pig and went first with his mock interview and his first quote was, "You know I really feel like, uh, you know…" The room immediately burst into laughter. Chris is an intelligent guy and has improved a great deal with his interviews by becoming a more articulate speaker. Perhaps I tried to sugarcoat it, but really that's what we try to do: sound educated and not speak the way we usually do. During the media training there were a few guys I was a little worried about. However, I was really impressed when I saw some of their interviews on TV and said to myself, "Wow, that didn't sound like us at all; it was good. Mission accomplished."

October 13, Practice Officially Starts

We can finally practice the way we want to. At 7 p.m. the NCAA officially allows us to start practice. Many people were asking if we would have a Midnight Madness practice, but Coach isn't a big fan of hoopla on our first practice night. I think if a creative idea came along he would be open to it, but he just wants to get started. I'll bet that if ESPN approached him about covering

UT Midnight Madness, he would do it for the exposure of our program.

Our first practice was open to the public, but there was no marketing scheme to publicize it. About 150-200 people showed up to watch. We knew what to expect because of the team individuals. Therefore, the first official practice was not as intimidating as it was in years past.

Practice went as expected except it was about an hour longer than we were accustomed to. With so many new players, Coach is still having to do tons of teaching, and at times this instruction takes away from the momentum of practice, but this instruction is important and must be done. I am now playing pretty well and it seems that some of my hard work is starting to pay dividends. As I watched some of my teammates struggle by grabbing their shorts after a drill or giving into fatigue during scrimmage, I found that I was better prepared than most for the first day of practice. The benefits from the Saturday mornings running "stadiums" with the weight vests and the extra conditioning were now kicking in.

With such a late practice, it was time for all of us to get to bed before practice in the morning. I forced myself to get into the ice cold whirlpool after practice. A goal of mine is to make myself get in the dreadfully cold whirlpool on a consistent basis after practice to try and prevent injury and soreness as much as possible.

October 14, Defense, Defense

Last night's practice was cut short because it was getting late and people needed to get their rest, but today there was no stopping Coach. We were scheduled to have Sunday off, so there was no reason for him not to kill us. Today, we were broken up into competitive teams and we focused primarily on the defensive end. Posted on each player's locker earlier in the week was a statistic which showed that we were 307ᵗʰ in the country in defensive field goals. 307ᵗʰ! That's ridiculous with the athletes we had, but Coach stressed that we have to be dedicated to improve our team defense. Many of our drills have a different scoring system than one might expect. Your team can only score with a stop on defense. Also, the only way you can get on defense is by scoring. If your team gets a stop you get to stay on defense until someone scores on you.

> Scoring System in Defensive Drills:
>> Steal or defensive rebound = 1 pt
>> Drawing a charge = 2 pts
>> Allowing an offensive rebound = -1 pt
>> Allowing a three point make = -1 pt

We usually play until a team gets four points, which doesn't sound like a lot, but with talented players on offense and point reductions for mistakes it can last a long time. Teams have to run as a consequence of losing. As a player, the best way to make a practice like this seem good is to win all the competitive drills. If you can win your drills and sip Gatorade while other teammates run, it makes you feel good.

By the end of practice there wasn't much left in anybody's tank. The coaches tell us that tonight is a good night to go out since we don't have practice tomorrow. But they have to know that we are so worn out that most of us will not want to go out. There was not much activity on campus because of fall break, and I hung out with Josh and Marques at the apartment. It's fun to hang out with guys off the court that have had the same kind of day you have had. They know how you feel. Actually, I am a little envious of the freshmen. They have such a great relationship and will develop lasting bonds during their careers and will become best friends. I'm close with my teammates, but being the lone senior I don't have a right-hand man or a longtime close player friend to share senior duties. Oh well, nothing is ever perfect.

October 18, Starting Five?

For the first time, Coach put together a lineup that could possibly be a starting five. With Wayne sitting out due to an ankle injury, the five players coach put together were Ramar, Duke, JaJuan, Chris and me. This seemed to be a very capable group, but as we played things did not go smoothly. We looked like an AAU team full of stars rather than a cohesive team. We had too many guys trying to do too much rather than playing within the offense. For the first time I worried about our on-court chemistry. It was frustrating to me, because when this type of play occurs I get lost in the mix. By the time I get the ball, I realize I have to be the one who runs the offense the way Coach wants it run. I like to be aggressive too, but I hold back because it isn't best for the team. As a result, the talented five we had together didn't gel and we were getting beat by the other group during scrimmage play.

Coach brought our five in a huddle and told us that this was the first day he had put a potential starting five together on the court and we weren't performing like starters. I was glad he pointed out the fact that we were playing too selfishly, and if we didn't learn how to play together then he will find a group of five that will. I wasn't totally disappointed because I know that with so many new players we need to be patient, but we will have to play better as a team if we want success.

October 19, One Downside of being a Student-Athlete

I knew that today was going to be tough. This is an example of a day in the life of a student-athlete that most other students wouldn't envy. I didn't get to bed until around 2 a.m. because I was working on a PowerPoint presentation that was due today. I had a five-page paper due in my first class at 8 a.m. and a 10-page paper due in my following class at 9:40 a.m., along with the PowerPoint presentation. Then I had to study for a quiz in my 12:40 class and also study for an exam for my Thursday night class. On top of this, I have basketball practice.

Needless to say, by the time I got to practice I was tired due to lack of sleep and mentally I was exhausted from my assignments and study. Perhaps, I could have avoided some of this if I didn't procrastinate completing my class assignments until the last minute. But that is just how I am. I get the job done and it's a competitive rush when you have to come through in the clutch with a deadline on a paper or a test.

I did my best to focus on the task at hand, which was a productive practice, but practice couldn't have gone worse. I played awfully. My shot wasn't falling, and my team got its butt kicked all day. I was on the losing team in every competitive drill, which led to extra running, and I felt like I was failing as a leader of my team.

As hard as I tried, nothing worked today. We continued to lose everything and I could tell Coach was disappointed in our group and especially in me. So, after one of the worst practices I can remember, the last thing I needed was an exam. I know that's a bad attitude but at that point, I couldn't have cared less about my schoolwork. I told myself that I sucked all day, but I had better not suck too badly on my test. I rushed to class, throwing on a T-shirt over my sweaty practice jersey. With tape still on my ankles from practice, I sat at my desk for the exam. Within seconds, a squadron of flies began to swarm around my sweaty shoes and feet. You know you stink when flies start buzzing you. Just another distraction as I crammed for the dreaded test. As sometimes happens, I knew the answers for the exam. It was in essay form, and for me to answer the questions thoroughly it required six handwritten pages. What a day!!

This day included the pressures of school assignments and the demands of basketball. I know school is more important, but I have to be honest and say that at this point in my career, a disappointing basketball day has a much greater impact than a test result. I can't help that basketball is the most important thing in my life behind God and family. For most athletes, few things are more important to them than their sport.

After my test, I went to night shooting and tried to work out my frustrations. That is the best medicine for me after a tough day on the court and stress from the classroom.

October 21, Another Bad Scrimmage

It's a big UT football game Saturday against Alabama and we have an open scrimmage this morning. There was a lot of activity and excitement on campus. We had real officials and it was going to be as game-like as possible. I needed to have a good day, because this was a big evaluation day for the coaches. More importantly, I needed a good day for my confidence.

We had several 10-minute segments of competition and would switch the teams up each time. It was very sloppy and only Duke and Ryan really stood out as having a big day. We just don't look in sync, which is somewhat expected this early in the season. I couldn't be more down about my play. I made some good hustle plays and some good passes but my shooting is still terrible. I went one for six from three-point range. Consistently, I can make seven out of 10 when I practice on my own, but then I freakin' go one for six when it counts. I have never been a consistently great shooter, yet it's the thing I work on most.

As I have said before, after a bad scrimmage, the last thing I feel like doing is rewarding myself with fun activities such as football games, tailgate parties, or going out at night.

For our team, as much talent as we have, I believe this will be a tougher team to coach than last year's team. I say this because expectations are higher and there is such a lack of experience on the court. Last year we had guys who had experienced basketball in the SEC and had gone through struggles that made us so hungry. Many of the new guys will have to learn throughout the year. With that said, it is too early to make any real assumptions, and I am sure that all of us will continue to improve and we will play better as a team in the weeks to come.

October 24, Player Evaluations

As we continue to scrimmage and prepare for the season, competition increases for playing time. Coach Pearl wants the players to know where they stand in that regard. Today, he addressed this in front of the team. Coach said that at this point, only JaJuan and Chris have separated themselves enough to have almost sure starting spots. Marques and Ramar are close at the point guard spot; Duke and Wayne are very close at the center spot; and Ryan and I are competing at forward. What many people don't realize is how much academic performance comes in to play in Coach Pearl's decision making. For example, if Marques and Ramar are neck and neck at the point guard position, then Coach will look to see which player is working the hardest academically to "break the tie."

The biggest surprise of these player evaluations came at my expense. Coach told the whole team that before practice started he thought I was a sure starter, but Ryan has closed the gap considerably. The way I have been playing compared to how Ryan has been playing, I was not surprised to hear this. That doesn't mean I liked hearing it. I'm the returning starting senior, yet my position is in jeopardy to a sophomore. The good thing about the team evaluations is that no one is letting this affect the team chemistry. It is great for the team that Ryan is playing well and I am happy for him. We need his consistency and effort. I have to step up to the challenge. This much competition will only make our team better and I don't want Ryan to start playing badly. I just have to play better than he does.

We all appreciate the communication Coach Pearl gives us regarding playing time. A player will know beforehand if he will be playing twenty minutes or five minutes. Whatever it is, it won't be a surprise. Using this approach, a player knows what to expect and knows how to prepare mentally and physically. This is an honest way to tell players where they stand. One key for coaches to get the best out of their players is not to play mind games with them; this is a way to avoid that.

October 25, SEC Media Day

Chris and I joined Coach Pearl on a flight to Birmingham for SEC Media Day. I was excited about the opportunity, but I'm constantly worried about my play and position. The media event was held at a hotel and there were several stages to go through. There was lunch before we began the interviews. After that we went into a room with our designated tables. Our table was in the same room as the Kentucky players and their coach, Tubby Smith. This room was for the print journalists and columnists. What I saw was amazing. Almost every reporter seemed to flock around Coach Pearl. I couldn't even see him because of the reporters huddled around him. Tubby Smith, a national championship coach at one of the greatest basketball universities in history, is sitting at a table nearby with maybe one or two reporters around him. By no means, is this a knock on Tubby Smith, but it sure demonstrates the public relations skills of Coach Pearl. He could have spoken for hours and they would have stayed glued to his every word. The passion and enthusiasm which he exudes make him a dynamic speaker.

Throughout the afternoon, we rotated to different rooms for television interviews for CSS, SEC-TV, Fox Sports, etc. It really was a cool experience. I can't get caught up in any of the media hoopla. I continue to get media exposure and writers compliment my game, but they don't realize how concerned I am with my play. I know the only opinion that truly matters is that of the coaching staff. So, I would be a fool to listen or worry about any other opinions or views.

We traveled back after a very long day out of town and we have a scrimmage at 7:30 p.m. Usually, I would have prepared by getting extra shots in before the scrimmage because I don't like being out of routine before play commences. The scrimmage went on and we looked much better than last time. We are all starting to get an idea of what Coach wants. Ryan and I both played well, so there was not much separation at that position. I was just happy to have a decent scrimmage. Things will continue to be interesting the next couple of weeks.

October 27, Coach Pearl's Coaches Clinic

About 250 high school coaches from surrounding areas were in town for Coach Pearl's clinic. Obviously, there is tremendous interest in how Coach Pearl runs a practice. It's an opportunity for coaches to learn how we run our press defense, see our drill work, and view some of our offensive and defensive principles. Every year, the coaches' clinic is a nervous practice for the players because we know we need to be sharp in everything we do. The last thing we want to do is embarrass our coach in front of other coaches. For some reason, maybe because of our youth, at the start we were not sharp. Coach was patient for a while but eventually he blew up on us. Coach was "mic'd" and usually a player would think their coach wouldn't blow up with visiting coaches in the stands. But Coach Pearl brings that same intensity every day regardless of who is in the stands. He even said it himself while screaming at us, "I'm not doing this because I have this microphone on; this is me every day, right?!" He doesn't change, and we all respect that.

Our practice continued to be sloppy, and eventually I huddled us up and said, "Look, Coach is really pissed but he isn't going to make us run sprints in front of these people because they paid to see a practice, but he is going to run the s#*@ out of us afterwards if we don't pick it up a notch. We still have time to save this and make it a decent practice. Let's go."

I'm not sure that helped, but practice did improve and I could tell it calmed Coach down. He complimented us at the end of practice for finishing strong, but emphasized that we can't have those bad lapses. We still ran at the end, but Coach said that it was not nearly as bad as he had planned to run us.

October 31, LeMoyne-Owen Magicians

Here we are, the first exhibition game. It does not have the same excitement as a regular season game, but everyone is anxious to start the season. We are playing a Division II school out of Memphis called LeMoyne-Owen. I know a couple of the players from their team since they are from my hometown.

One of the players is Taurean Moy a.k.a. "T-Head." T-Head is a Memphis high school basketball legend. He was two years ahead of me and went to a school named Booker T. Washington. He is best known for, get this, an 84-point performance while connecting on twenty-four three pointers in one game. T-Head was an amazing shooter and player but got in trouble with the law and has spent the last few years in the Nebraska State Penitentiary.

Rumor has it that T-Head scored 72 points in the Penitentiary League Championship game before being released the following week and joining LeMoyne-Owen. So, I have been joking with our team this weekend with threats of what the legendary T-Head will do by saying things like, "He hit 72 in prison, man. He isn't scared of us; good luck whoever is guarding him."

I saw T-Head before the game and we had a chance to catch up and he said, "Yeah, I'm playing all right but I just don't have any legs, I'm not in shape." I could understand why he wasn't in great shape given his situation. Anyway, we don't take any teams lightly but we all know in the back of our minds that we should win this one rather easily. With that said, everyone still has butterflies as many of our players will be making their collegiate debut.

I am nervous for different reasons and the problem is that the game I love so much and have been playing my whole life is not fun for me right now. That's when you know there is a problem. Right now, I'm extremely uptight, frustrated and my confidence is low. Then all of a sudden, it seemed like there was a messenger sent to tell me to relax and appreciate what I have. A young boy named Cody was brought into the locker room and he had obviously had some tough health issues that no child should go through. Apparently, he was my number one fan and when I met him, it had a calming effect on me. I got a shoe out of my locker and signed it for him. I wish I could have done more, but I could tell this simple gesture meant a lot to him.

The game went on and we blew them away. T-Head was two-of-fourteen for three-point attempts, so I guess he still hasn't gotten his legs back. I played well but only scored three points. In blowout victories, I usually get lost in the mix as everyone boosts their individual stats. Still I played decently and it is tough for anyone to get much out of a 60-point victory.

November 3, Tusculum Pioneers

It's our last exhibition before the regular season as we face Tusculum. This is a better, more structured opponent, so we were hoping to learn more about our team through this game. They played with us for a while, but eventually our press and fast-paced style paid off and we went on to a large victory. As for me, I planned on being a little more aggressive offensively. Then I ended the game with three points on three field goal attempts. I'm trying my best to find my niche with the team, but I can't seem to get comfortable on the court. I think a lot of that has to do with playing point guard most of my life and being the pass-first type of player who is happy with just running the offense smoothly and getting a win. I need to get the swagger and confidence that are necessary for me to play at my best, and I need to find that by Friday.

November 4, Being Humbled

It was nice to have an easy Saturday and have a light practice. There is a home football game, so I got together with family and friends for a tailgate party, which helped take my mind off basketball for a while. It is also nice to be around guys who have always been my friends who couldn't care less about how well I play. For example one family friend, Mike King, said, "Hell, if I'm going to drive up and watch you play; your butt better score more points than you have fouls." (I finished with three points and four fouls last night). This may seem a little harsh, but all of us need Mike Kings in our lives.

November 6, Practice for Middle Tennessee State University

There was a new sense of urgency and a serious attitude in practice as we begin to prepare for the first regular season game against Middle Tennessee State University (MTSU). There was a much more business-like approach in practice. This is a risky game to schedule. MTSU is a smaller instate school, so we are expected to win big. If we don't accomplish this, MTSU has a moral victory; thus it's somewhat of a no-win situation for us. Also, a number of the MTSU players feel like they were snubbed by UT in the recruiting process and will play with chips on their shoulders. In addition these guys are excellent players, well coached and have prepared all summer for us. They see Tennessee as the first game of their season and it would make their year to upset us. We have to do everything we can to avoid an early season upset.

With all that said, I'm not sure our younger guys realize the focus and concentration required for each opponent to succeed at this level. Practice was sloppy and the players did not measure up to the coaches' sense of urgency. It's common knowledge what a fiery guy Coach Pearl is and how he can really get in your face and wear you out. Some think that must be the most intimidating thing for his players. But the complete opposite is the truth; nothing strikes more fear in the players than Coach Pearl's silent frustration. He has "that look." If Bruce Pearl is lost for words, we must have really done something terrible.

As we practiced up and down the court, it was turnover after turnover, missed layups, missed box-outs and we were waiting for him to erupt. But he just stood there silent as a sphinx and let us continue to screw up. I guess this is a teaching method. When he eventually stopped play, there was dead silence. I figured he would put the balls up and tell us to get on the baseline for sprints. Surprisingly, he calmly explained that we need to come every day to get better and not just survive practice.

For awhile Coach Pearl has reminded us of how bad it will feel in the locker room, if we lose to teams like MTSU. For example, if a player misses a box-out, he might say, "What if that is the game winning rebound and MTSU just got it. How are you going to feel in the locker room after that? Is it worth that feeling of a loss? Or should we suck it up and successfully make each play in order to taste the feeling of victory?"

Practice definitely ended on a down note, because we didn't have a good one. Hopefully, the message was sent clearly that we need a different mentality in practice.

November 8, Some Finer Points of the Game

Today was a much better, more productive practice. One problem we have with so many players who were former superstars of their high school team is, they are not used to being corrected. Perhaps these players were so good in high school that their coaches let them do whatever they wanted. When Coach Pearl corrects them, they get down on themselves and wonder, "Why is Coach on my case?" Some players can take the harsh criticism, while others can't. None of the players have reacted negatively to Coach, but they get down on themselves because they aren't used to being reminded they are less than perfect. The difference between high school and Division I collegiate basketball is gigantic; there is so much to learn. In my fourth season, I feel like I am finally beginning to fully grasp what basketball is and how it is played; screens, stances, angles, etc. As a team, it sure involves a lot more than just putting the ball in the hole.

Duke actually nicknamed me "Coach," which I take as a huge compliment. I even watch basketball in a different way. Watching on television, I don't see 10 guys running around and watch Dwayne Wade drive to the basket for a dunk. I see what led to that. I see Wade was given a screen and the opponent gave a soft hedge on the screen, leaving his defender unable to recover and the backside had some action to occupy the help side defense, leading to an open dunk for Wade. As my knowledge of the game increases, my thoughts about coaching in the future also increase.

November 9, Scouting Our Opponent

A very light practice was held the day before the game as we get plenty of shots up and walk through the opponent's plays. Coach Forbes is designated to present the scouting report. He spends hours breaking down film and dissecting our opponent. He teams with Coach Pearl as they go over MTSU personnel and plays.

Our walk-ons have one of the hardest jobs because they are our scout team and have to learn the opponent's plays, out-of-bounds plays, press breaks, defenses, etc., all in a couple days.

The day before the game, Coach likes to have the scout team lightly jog through the plays as we defend them to avoid any injuries the day before a game. He can really get irritated if the speed picks up too fast.

Steven Pearl is red-shirting this year and making the most of this year to get better. He is working hard and doing everything he can to compete for next season. However, for now, he is on the scout team and he was frustrated at the fact that he had to only go half speed. I was standing near him and he said, "Screw it, I'm going hard."

I warned him not to do it because Coach was going to yell at him, but he said he didn't care. So at that point I dared him by saying, "Well, get the ball and drive it real hard and shoot it and see what happens." I couldn't believe it, but he did just that and I could see Coach's face get red. Within seconds he said, "Slow the hell down. You got that, Pearl? I call the shots around here!" I wanted to laugh as I knew it was going to happen. For one thing, it shows that Coach treats his son on an equal footing with the other players.

Section II — Season Play

T he months of preseason preparation come to an end today, because at 7:30 p.m. tonight at Thompson-Boling Arena we will have our first official game of the season. Our first opponent is the Middle Tennessee State University Blue Raiders from Murfreesboro, Tennessee. Before regular season play is finished, we are scheduled to play thirty-one games against major universities. Many of these games will be against teams ranked among the top 25 NCAA Division I teams in the country. Six of these games will be against teams who made it to last year's Elite Eight. These teams are Florida (twice), LSU, Memphis, Ohio State and Texas.

Sixteen of our games will be against SEC teams. We are the defending SEC East champions and eagerly look forward to the opportunity of defending our championship. This is one of our team goals. Other goals are to play well in the SEC postseason tournament and be selected to play in the NCAA postseason tournament and advance at least to the Sweet 16. In other words, we want to be active and successful participants in what has come to be called: March Madness. So let season play begin!

November 10, Middle Tennessee State University Blue Raiders

Finally, it's here. Game day. I haven't slept well because of excitement and anxiety but it's a good feeling and the right feeling to have before a game. There is such a huge difference between getting pumped for a real game rather than an exhibition game. I know you should have the same excitement for every opponent, but it is human nature to be more excited about a game that counts. In addition this is the last season opener of my college career.

We go to the gym for walkthroughs at 2:30 p.m. which consists of getting up shots and free throws and going through the opponent's plays one last time. This is very casual and players are dressed in their sweats or shorts and a T-shirt. We have our pregame meal at 3:30 p.m., four hours before tip-off. This is essentially the same routine we will have before every game.

Today we had a special guest. The legendary Allan Houston was in the house. Allan is one of the greatest to ever play at the University of Tennessee. He was also an NBA All-star and an American Olympic team gold medalist. He ate the pregame meal with us and everyone tries to act real cool. But soon we start acting like little kids, looking up to a superstar.

Allan patiently and politely answered each question we asked about the NBA and his life and activities. He has done what we dream to accomplish. Allan is more than an NBA player; he is one of the more well-known, more involved Christians in the NBA. So, after the pregame meal some of us followed him into the locker room for a devotional. It was very informal and Allan didn't have anything written down, but you could tell how experienced he was at leading groups in religious discussions. He spoke about how in his early years he wanted nothing to do with the Bible or the Lord. He warned us how easy it is to get caught up in the hype with so many people around you telling you how great you are, and advised us to stay grounded and humble and to focus on what really matters in life. He told us "There is more to life than this," and that tons of people are considered "good guys"; that's easy, he was a "good guy," but the key is, does God consider you righteous? Are you just a good person or are you a good, righteous person? Some of us may be on the bench right now, but we can work hard through the Lord's word to play an important role. In closing, he told us that God blesses obedience. If we discipline ourselves and do our best to live in a Godly manner, then we will be blessed. Allan Houston impressed me beyond belief. If a preacher or chaplain gave the same message, we would have listened, but Allan Houston, talking to basketball players, made it much more effective. The University of Tennessee should be extremely proud to call Allan Houston an alumnus.

In some ways the game itself was anti-climatic, we almost doubled their score by halftime, taking a 45 to 27 lead. The final score was 83 to 52. We had five players who scored in double digits. Everyone played extremely well. To be honest, we looked better than I expected. Coach told us, "It takes a lot to impress me, but that effort impressed me."

November 12, NIT Season Tip-Off Tournament Games

We arrived in Nashville to battle three other teams (Belmont, Fordham, and UNC-Wilmington) for the right to go to Madison Square Garden and play for the NIT Season Tip-Off Tournament championship. There were 16 teams invited to participate in this prestigious tournament, and we were proud to be representing our University and the SEC.

We went straight to the gym for shoot around. We typically get plenty of shots up to get ourselves adjusted to the rims and court. Coach doesn't like to go over too many plays or defensive schemes anywhere other than our home court in fear of someone taking notes about our game plans, which we call an "eye in the sky." An entertaining part of this day happened at dinner.

The University takes good care of us and we are well fed. On the road, we may have something catered at the hotel or go out to a nice restaurant. Tonight we went to an elegant restaurant. Before I poke a little fun, I must recognize that all of our players, including this senior, have been exposed to different situations and that each of us knows and are aware of things that the others haven't been exposed to. Our meal tonight illustrated that fact, as one of our guys ordered ranch dressing for his Caesar salad, not realizing the dressing was already on the salad. This confused the waiter who dutifully brought a side of ranch dressing. For dinner, I ordered a filet mignon stuffed with bleu cheese. This sounded appetizing to another one of our guys who said "I'll take the same thing except I want mine stuffed with ranch." "Uh, sir, we don't really have ranch that we stuff our steaks with," the confused waiter responded. Our player, in turn, was confused because the waiter had just brought out a side of ranch and then said they didn't have any ranch. Finally one of the guys ordered a ribeye. As we waited on our food, I said something like, "This may take a while since we all ordered steak." The player who ordered the ribeye responded, "You're the ones who ordered steak." I said, "What are you talking about? You ordered the ribeye." "Yeah, ribs!" he said confidently. After we gathered our breath from laughing so hard, we explained that ribeye was a type of steak not ribs. He was able to laugh with us and at himself about the whole thing. Don't believe for a minute that we are a team of dummies. We just have some guys who are inexperienced when it comes to dining at nice restaurants. And, our basketball experiences provide a lot of learning opportunities for all of us outside the realm of basketball.

There was plenty of laughter on the bus, as we headed back to the hotel. This is a great bunch of guys to be associated with. Hopefully, we can get serious and focused for our game tomorrow.

November 13, Fordham Rams

Sloppy, sloppy, sloppy describes our game with Fordham. We committed twenty-six turnovers, but Fordham topped us with 29 turnovers as we got after them with our press. Throw in 51 personal fouls and it's easy to see why "sloppy" is the best word to describe this contest. We finally prevailed, winning with a 78 to 71 score.

Fordham couldn't stop Chris as he poured in 30 points on nine-of-16 field goal attempts and seven-of-eight free throws.

Tomorrow night we will play UNC-Wilmington, an 88-83 winner over Belmont. The winner of that game will represent the South in matches with the winners of the East, West and North regions at Madison Square Garden.

November 14, UNC-Wilmington Seahawks

At 8 p.m. we have an opportunity to earn our way to Madison Square Garden. It's a quick turnaround—less than twenty-four hours after last night's victory. The coaches stressed the importance of us getting off our feet and getting plenty of rest. We went through the same routine as yesterday as far as walkthrough and pregame meals are concerned. We really have to focus on the opponents scouting report, because there is no time to practice against our scout team. Therefore, we pay close attention to the film. It is tough to gain a good understanding of a team that you see for the first time via film. But you try to get familiar with them and it helps. By the third time we walked through plays and watched the break down film, we have it down reasonably well and have a fair recognition of their plays.

I got a nice nap before we headed to the gym and my body feels good considering the back-to-back games. I'm trying to put last night's game behind me and hopefully put together a solid effort tonight. Like Coach says, some nights particular players will play well and others won't so maybe some of us can turn around and play better tonight.

We arrived at the arena and waited for the consolation game to finish. I felt bad for Belmont and Fordham because it's tough to get up for a consolation type game. It exposes a team's character, because, given the circumstances, it is easy to just pack it in. We all talked about how glad we were that we didn't have to play the consolation game.

We took the court and got off to a good start but couldn't protect the lead. Again, we weren't able to deliver that final blow we were looking for. We led 42-40 at halftime. After half-time intermission and during the second half we turned it on and put it to them. Our style of play caught up to them and they ended the game with 29 turnovers. JaJuan lit it up after being a little off the night before. He played his heart out. He was all over the place and when he gets into a rhythm he gives our team so much on both ends of the court. Chris paced the way with 17 points and it's always nice to have such a reliable player. Josh Tabb was huge off the bench with his defense and the way he attacked pressure. He was another guy coming off a mediocre performance yet turned out to be an unsung hero. The story of the night is Ryan Childress' continued excellent play. He was unbelievable tonight making threes, capturing offensive rebounds, and making good decisions. I didn't even score. When I was out of the game, the team played better and that really hurt my pride. Here I am, the senior, the captain, the so called "leader," and I don't even score. I am giving my best effort and that's all I can ask, but what the hell is going on with me? The reality, though, is that this is a great sign for our team because it shows that we have enough depth for different players to pickup the slack when others have off nights. There was a positive atmosphere in the locker room with a lot of high fivin' and huggin' going on.

November 19, Coppin State Eagles

This was more or less a tune up game before we head to Madison Square Garden. The big danger here, as often happens, is looking past your opponent. Personally, I need to have a good game for my confidence.

We ran out for warm-ups and the energy wasn't there. There were barely any fans in the stands, and we could tell this was a game that we should easily handle.

We started off slow and sluggish as our lack of focus would have predicted. Coach wasn't looking past this opponent and he expressed his disappointment in our energy level and execution. As previously mentioned, some of the younger players are fragile when coach corrects them. Tonight, coach had enough of their immature behavior. He yelled, "The next player who pouts, puts their head down, or shows a negative attitude when I'm trying to coach and teach won't play the rest of the game." He carried his anger into the locker room and questioned his relationship with us, "Do we not have a good enough relationship where I can teach you and try and help you? Maybe not. I thought we were cooler than this and good enough friends to be in this together. If I ask you to go in the game for one play all game, you better give me 100 percent. Don't you think I would do it for you if the situation was reversed? Damn right I would." The message was clear we needed to stop feeling sorry for ourselves and accept the individual roles Coach thought was best for the team. It was an eventful halftime.

We went on to a large sized victory and our body language improved. Some news of the second half was that I got a dunk!! That's right, I dunked! I got a steal at half court and went down with a one hand dunk. It was my first college career dunk and it was nice to show some people who didn't think I was capable of doing that. Bob Kesling helped me out a bit as he called the game over the radio. With my siblings listening, Kesling called the play emphatically, "Bradshaw with a tomahawk dunk!" A tomahawk comes off like a Michael Jordan dunk, but I'll take it. Of course, one of my brothers who was listening left me a nice message, "Tomahawk? Yeah, right. I'm gonna have to see the tape of this before I believe that." You didn't fool my brother, but thanks for the effort Mr. Kesling.

November 20-21, Madison Square Garden Here We Come

We had a light practice as we went over the scouting report for Butler. Before practice we had an unusual guest in our locker room. Mary Mahoney, a dining etiquette expert, came to prepare us for our scheduled dinner at Tavern on the Green in New York City with a mini-etiquette class. I'm not sure if this came as a result of the dinner stories from Nashville. It was very informative, though, and we all learned some new things. It is funny if you think about all of us in a dining etiquette class, but it was helpful and now hopefully we are prepared for New York on and off the court.

November 21 was one morning that none of us minded setting our alarms for 6:30 a.m. We didn't mind because we were getting on an early flight to New York City for an unbelievable experience and opportunity to play in Madison Square Garden. I was one of only two players who had ever been to The Big Apple, so it is going to be fun watching a bunch of Southerners experience New York City for the first time.

The plane landed in New York and Chris asked me if we were in the same time zone as Knoxville. I couldn't pass up the opportunity to play a little joke, so I told him we were on mid-Eastern time, which meant we were an hour later than Knoxville. Chris just said "All right." "Yeah," I responded, "I hate this time zone because Monday Night Football doesn't come on until about 10:30." I left it there and Chris continued to think we were in a different time zone.

Chris, JaJuan, and I stepped off the plane and got into a limo to head to a press conference. We were thrilled about getting to ride in a limo until about 10 more people piled in, making it an uncomfortable ride. We didn't complain because we were too excited to be there. The press conference was in the hotel and it wasn't a huge setting but the atmosphere was impressive. I was introduced and had a chance to speak with Myles Brand, head of the NCAA. I introduced myself to Steve Lavin, ESPN analyst, because he coached Andre Patterson at UCLA before Andre transferred to UT. Then, I had a chance to speak with Jerod Haase, assistant coach at North Carolina, who I mentioned earlier. Jerod was the former Kansas player who wrote a book similar to what I am trying to accomplish. I had spoken on the phone with him before, but it was nice to be formally introduced. Finally, I had a lengthy sit-down interview with Stacey Dales, sideline reporter with ESPN. This was all one after the other and I was amazed at the people I was mingling with and having casual conversations with. JaJuan said, "As cool as this scene is, imagine the Final Four." There's a thought.

From there we hurried to practice. We arrived at an old building and had to go up several flights of steps before finding a small court with dusty floors. "Where the heck did they bring us?" we asked. Come to find out we were at the prestigious New York Athletic Club, where there was so much history. Suddenly everyone had a newfound respect for the small, old, dirty gym floor. We practiced hard during our allotted time, then we had to hustle up and shower for dinner.

We put on our best clothes and made our way to the famous Tavern on the Green. The atmosphere was unbelievable at the restaurant with crystal chandeliers and winding, narrow pathways, almost maze like, to the different rooms. All four teams were there as we sat down to a wonderful five-course meal. A few short speeches were made since this was somewhat of a kickoff for the tournament. I thought we handled ourselves well in the formal setting. We didn't have to apply too much of our etiquette training, but some of us learned a little more about fine dining.

After dinner it was still early so we watched some film and walked around the city for a couple hours before curfew. It was fun to watch guys who had never been to the city before and were amazed at the bustle and busyness of New York. A few of the guys said that it was just like the movies. We had our little social time and headed to bed to take care of business tomorrow before playing Butler.

November 22, Madison Square Garden and the Butler Bulldogs

We left for shoot around thirty minutes early so we could stop and walk around Rockefeller Center and see that area. We took some neat pictures, but had to make it quick because of shoot around. All the players kept saying how they wished they could come to New York sometime without worrying about basketball. But because of basketball we were able to go to the highlight of our trip, Madison Square Garden. We walked through the historic halls of MSG and, although we had tons of respect for where we were, we had no idea of the history in this building.

We went into the Knick's locker room and finally hit the floor that we had all been anticipating. Immediately we began imitating the Bulls versus Knicks games' highlights that we grew up watching. It was amazing to be playing on the same floor as all of the players we wanted to be like. I know we weren't playing an NBA game, but playing any game in Madison Square Garden is enough to give you goose bumps.

The excitement and energy in our team were there and we seemed to have the right focus. Butler is a team that has already beaten Notre Dame and Indiana and is very dangerous. We know they have the poise and patience to potentially take us out of our game. We thrive on opponents' turnovers and they average only eight turnovers a game. They consistently take the shot clock all the way down until the very end and they are outstanding on defense. We knew they were very, very tough.

Tipoff arrived and defensively, we started off great. We were executing to perfection and were off to a 21-8 lead, thanks to JaJuan, who started the game with three quick three-pointers. We had the team scouted well and looked to be on our way, but we didn't deliver the knockout blow, and from our 21-8 lead, it was all downhill. We couldn't have been uglier offensively as we ended the first half with 14 turnovers. What was once a 13-point lead was trimmed to a three-point lead at halftime. More importantly Butler had taken our confidence and momentum. It didn't get any better as we embarrassed ourselves by shooting an unbelievable three for 29 in the second half. That must be some type of negative record. We missed layups, free throws, and open threes. It felt similar to last year's tournament loss to Wichita State, a team we were supposed to beat, yet we let the opportunity slip by. Coach said after the game that it was too simple to blame our loss just on our shooting. Of course he's right. There were other factors. But shooting 10 percent was an enormous factor. To make things worse, as our locker room was silent and we had our heads down, we heard the Butler players, across the hall in their locker room, chanting and singing their fight song.

Coach didn't erupt like I thought he might, but his points got across. He preached to us to keep faith in what we do in our system and in our abilities.

The following game was Gonzaga versus the heavily favored North Carolina. We all had high hopes of making it to the championship game to face North Carolina. However, North Carolina, the number two team in the country, was upset tonight and we would face them in the consolation game. So, at least, we still get to play North Carolina. It just happens to be the 4:30 p.m. consolation game. This is still an unbelievable opportunity and we better get our minds right or we will get embarrassed by an extremely talented and well-coached team.

November 23 was Thanksgiving Day, but it wasn't the Thanksgiving we wanted. The Macy's parade went through town but it was raining. It was almost representative of our game last night, because a Butler rainstorm definitely came down on our parade. Coach reminded us to be thankful for everything we have and he said the way we handle this adversity will reveal our character. He said that anyone can sail a ship when the winds are calm, but what happens when things get rough is a real measure of character.

We turned our attention to North Carolina. The coaches began scouting them as soon as we lost and were up late into the night and up early in the morning. Too often, the time and effort the coaches put into trying to make us successful goes unnoticed and unappreciated. They spend countless hours trying to find ways to put us in positions to succeed and their work ethic is unprecedented.

We went to the New York Athletic Club for shoot around and went over the scouting report. As great as North Carolina is, they really are not that difficult to scout because they do not run too many set plays. They are extremely well-coached but one of their strong suits is they depend on their players being better than the other team's. And with their talent that approach works.

November 24, North Carolina Tar Heels

We aren't treating this like a third-place tournament game. This is an opportunity to play the number-two ranked team in the country in Madison Square Garden. We followed our normal routines throughout the day and got on the bus and headed to MSG. If you can't get pumped up for this one, then you shouldn't be playing the game. Energy and excitement surrounded us. It reminded me of the feeling just before a high school game against a cross town rival. During warm-ups, I reflected for a moment and just thanked God for so many blessings.

The game started and we weren't playing that poorly but North Carolina stretched their lead to 20 points by halftime. Most teams would be shut down, but you wouldn't believe the energy in our locker room. You would have thought we were leading by 20; it was crazy. We are confident and feel we can overcome anything and anyone. We came out in the second half and cut the deficit to 12 points, but couldn't get over the hump. Still that half of basketball was one of the proudest halves of basketball I have been privileged to play. The heart, intensity and passion we showed through adversity were admirable. We came together and it was all about the team.

The true rallying point came about midway through the second half. JaJuan Smith was called for an intentional foul and ejected from the game. A terrible call and because of it, we lost a key player. JaJuan was keeping us within striking distance and he is such a competitor. I hated to see him forced to leave the game and have no control of the outcome because I know how badly he wanted to play. When that call was made, the rest of the team sucked it up and came together as if it was us against the world. We fought to the very end but came up short. The talent on the other side made plays that we just couldn't stop; natural ability took its toll. This gave us a taste of what a national championship caliber team looks like. As one ESPN analyst said, "They don't have a lot of plays, but they have a lot of players that make plays." Too much talent can be one of coaching's greatest challenges, but Roy Williams does a great job with their program. I had an opportunity to talk to Coach Williams at the Tavern on the Green, because of his connection to Buzz Peterson, my former coach, in the North Carolina family. Anyway, after the game he shook my hand firmly and leaned into my ear and said, "You're a great competitor and I have a tremendous respect for you." I know he was being kind, yet it will be one of the fondest memories of my career. I had a solid game with 10 points, seven assists, and five steals, but was overmatched down low by future NBA players Brandan Wright and Tyler Hansbrough, who mostly had their way with me.

In the locker room there was disappointment but also positive vibes due to the toughness and heart we displayed. Coach spoke of how proud he was of us, but also reminded us of poor practices in the past that may have affected the outcome of the game. However, he reiterated how proud he was of us and our efforts.

I was called into the press-conference room and Coach Pearl was already answering questions. I walked in right as he said, "You know, Dane Bradshaw might not get any Naismith National Player of the Year votes, but I'm not sure I would trade him for anyone in the country." Now, I can think of quite a few All-Americans that coach would want to consider, but that's beside the point. Those words made me feel better after a hard-fought loss.

Overall, we came to New York and lost two games. Certainly, this was not what we wanted to do. The Butler Bulldogs end up winning the tournament. But we gained some valuable experience and learned, when we play like a team, we are capable of competing with any college team.

November 25-26, Hurt Again

Not sure how to date this because I'm sitting here at 4 a.m. wide awake watching SportsCenter. I can't sleep because I have injuries to both shoulders and it hurts to lie on either side. It's pretty tough sleeping straight up; not to mention I'm sorely pissed about my latest injuries, especially to my right shoulder. I have a muscle stimulation unit that trainer Chad gave me to bring home from practice so I could continue rehab. I apply a pad to the injured area and allow the stimulation to work in about 30-minute intervals. Because my shoulders are hurting badly, primarily my right one, I want to do as much treatment as possible so I can be ready to play Monday night.

My left shoulder was injured in our loss to Butler when my arm was pulled back awkwardly while reaching high to snag a ball. It hurt to raise my arm past shoulder height, but that's not a huge concern because my right arm is much more important. However, somehow I managed to injure my right shoulder in our game against North Carolina. I don't really remember doing it, but it probably happened toward the end of the game when I dove for a loose ball and my right arm ended up on the bottom of a pile of players scrambling after the ball. This seems like the obvious reason, but it didn't hurt until the next morning when I couldn't raise my arm in front of me without sharp pain.

We had a very light practice that consisted of shots and watching film of our next opponent, Louisiana-Lafayette. I tried to shoot, but it hurt way too badly and I spent all of the practice with Chad doing treatment on it. I think it may be strained biceps tendons on both shoulders.

We had a short practice scheduled before getting on the plane to Louisiana. I knew it was best that I try to rest my shoulders as much as possible, but I didn't want to sit out of practice. However, Coach made the decision for me and told me to rest and treat my shoulders. He knows the importance of practicing, but realizes that sometimes trying to get healthy is more important than practice.

We left for Louisiana and arrived to 80-degree weather. It was a nice change from having to wear our sweats everywhere. I continued to do treatment with Chad in hopes that I would have a significant improvement in my shoulders for game day.

November 27, Louisiana-Lafayette Rajun Cajuns

The big news of the day was a change in the starting lineup. Coach decided he was going to start Jordan over Ramar at the point guard spot. He was hoping that we could get off to better starts at the beginning of games and the beginning of the second half as well. Defense was also a factor as Ramar is still learning some of our defensive principles. A huge factor that gave Jordan the nod was a stat that we keep up with called the plus/minus chart. For example, if I check into the game and the score is 32-32 then come out of the game with the score 40-32 in our favor, this would be +8 for me. If the opponent would have gained a lead, my number would be negative number. This is a measurement of how well the team does while you are on the court. In Jordan's case, we recently lost to North Carolina by 14 but he had a +5 score, meaning we won by five points while Jordan was on the court. Coach took this into consideration and it helped Jordan earn a starting position. Ramar's attitude was good and hopefully this will affect him in a positive way. As we lined up at walkthrough to practice a jump ball situation, Jordan didn't know where to stand because it had been three or four years since he had been on the court for an actual tip off. We all laughed hard at his hilarious antics as he joked, "What is this? Jump ball? I didn't know they still did this. It has been a while for me."

I started thinking about my starting five predictions at the beginning of the fall. It was Ramar, Chris, me, Wayne and Major. Look how many things have happened since then and how wrong I was. Seven games into the season and the lineup consists of Jordan, Chris, JaJuan, me and Duke. I always knew JaJuan would find his way there, as he is such a great player. It is interesting to see how many changes have taken place in a short period and we still have so far to go.

We are set for tipoff at 7 p.m. and the stands aren't packed. They sell beer at the games here and we are amidst the Rajun Cajun fans. The fans were brutal as we lined up for the national anthem. One fan yelled to us, "Raise your hand if you know who your father is?" and "Steven Pearl! I wonder how you got on the team!" The game hasn't even started and we are getting hard heat from the fans.

My shoulders were greased up with all types of Flex-All type creams and I took some extra-strength muscle relaxers, so I was feeling OK. For some reason, Coach designed a play that would leave me open for a three-point shot to start off the game. I laughed and thought, "I can barely lift my arms over my shoulders and for the first time in my career this guy is calling for a three-point shot by me to start the game." We pushed the ball up the court and I faked a screen for Chris and sprinted to the open spot where I was left wide open. Bang! I nailed it and couldn't help but laugh running back on defense. Of course, when I got back to the bench the players informed me that I need to hurt my shoulders more often. We had a big lead, but let them back in it because we were not able to deliver the final blow. This has become a lousy trademark of our team.

The relatively small crowd got extremely loud as Louisiana-Lafayette made a big run. By the second half, beer sales made 5,000 fans sound like 10,000. However, Chris Lofton got back on track and carried us with 31 points. We pulled it out down the stretch in a tough game, and the players that finished the game in the tight situation were Jordan, Josh, Chris, Wayne, and me. Our strength coach, Troy Wills, pointed this out because he was proud of the fact that four of those five were consistent participators in the Saturday morning stadium runs this off-season.

Road wins are sweet. Hearing a silent crowd as you walk off in celebration is neat for a team winning on the road. My former English teachers might call "Hearing a silent crowd" an oxymoron. I sure hope we get to experience a lot of these oxymorons when SEC play starts. The best part of a road win may be the fun atmosphere on the flight home. Everyone is hyper, laughing, and talking, instead of moping about a loss.

We got home about 2 a.m. and I have to be up in five hours to work on a nine-page exam that has to be turned in by noon. I was happy about our win, but sure dreaded the work involved with my upcoming exam.

November 29, Studying Murray State Film

It is important to me to feel like I outwork and out-prepare my opponents. My bad shoulders are hindering the outwork part of my routine. Our next game is against Murray State.

Since I can't outwork the Murray State players, I decided to compensate by studying more film on their play, hoping to gain an extra edge. In place of night shooting, I borrowed the breakdown tape of Murray State. The breakdown tape is a compilation of the other team's offensive sets and play calls. This is what we view together as a team in the film room. The coach in charge of the particular scouting effort watches games of the opponent and chooses which plays and tendencies we need to pay attention to. Jason Schneider is our principal video coordinator. He edits the tape and puts together the breakdown film organized with clips of each player, the offensive sets, how they break the press, out-of-bounds plays, and how they play defense. It is an in-depth evaluation of the opponent and every coaching staff does this in an attempt to strategize effectively. Schneider is another hard worker on Pearl's staff. Usually, the coaches know the scout better than the players do, but we practice the scout enough times to where we have a reasonably clear idea going into the game.

Tonight, I sat at my apartment with ice on my shoulders and closely studied the breakdown tape. The player I am assigned to guard is Shawn Witherspoon, who was the preseason pick for Player of the Year in his conference—the Ohio Valley Conference. He is a talented player who played very well against us last year and is the main focus of our scout.

I wrote down his tendencies, such as where he was on particular plays, and looked for the best way to defend him. After I studied the film, I quizzed myself. For example, I would say, "If number 22 starts on the left wing, what play are they trying to run?" A player may start at the same spot all the time, but you can still see some things he may do to tip off the play. Hopefully, this can get me some steals, or at least I can take away their play, which can be just as effective.

As I sat there immersed in the study of the breakdown tape, the thought of becoming a coach after my playing days crept into my mind. I love the competitiveness and strategy behind it all. Also, I have learned so much about the game under Coach Pearl and other coaches that I think I could be a successful coach. But that is not my immediate concern; tomorrow we play the Murray State Racers and we will see if my extra study helps us.

November 30, Murray State Racers

We started the game playing well. I don't need to score much to be happy. I just need to be involved and feel like I'm contributing. I was able to do that with some rebounds, steals, assists and a few easy buckets, scoring 12 points. The +/- system I explained earlier was in my favor.

There were a few tight moments throughout the game but we extended the lead and easily won the game. As for my opponent Witherspoon, he finished the game 0-6 from the floor, four points, and four fouls. Of course, foul trouble got him out of his rhythm, but I know I helped make it tough on him by disrupting the play calls. I felt prepared on the floor and felt like I knew what was coming. Not only could I beat my man to his spot on the court, but I could yell to my teammates so that they would know what was coming. It made us better as a team defensively. I definitely benefitted from my breakdown tape study and plan to continue to do that.

December 3-4, Practice for Memphis

Practice was at 10 a.m. and we began as if we had just rolled out of bed, which most of us probably had. We continued to try to get the energy and tempo up, but the practice was just sluggish. To make things worse, we are trying to prepare for Memphis and, right now, the player focus is not there. Eventually, the practice got so bad that Coach Pearl decided to make us run as punishment for the rest of practice.

Even though we started and ended on a sour note, Coach still found a way to put a positive, motivational spin on things as we left practice. Hopefully, we can put this behind us because we need to prepare for Memphis as best we can.

It's December 4 and practice was much more productive today. Hopefully, this plus the energy and excitement of tomorrow's game will help carry us to victory.

December 5, Memphis Tigers

This is a very important game for our Tennessee Volunteer basketball team. We are playing a team ranked number 17 in the nation. Right now they are our top instate rival, thus Tennessee bragging rights and instate recruiting are all factors. The game will be on national television, so it is a golden opportunity to showcase our team.

Personally, there may not be a bigger game on the schedule for me. Memphis is my hometown and you always want to earn the respect of your hometown friends and fans. Last year at Memphis I had a career high with 21 points and 10 rebounds, but we lost. With a win tonight, I can go home with my head held high. No matter what anyone says or thinks, athletes deeply care how they are perceived at home.

To start the game, I had three good looks from three-point land, but missed all of them, which was frustrating. Fortunately, Chris Lofton is on our team. Memphis simply had no one who could guard him. Threes, layups, free throws; he scored every which way. He truly was proving to be an All-American with his play. Chris' shot making combined with our team's stellar defense helped us jump to an astonishing 43-22 halftime lead. But we know that all great teams will make a run and Memphis gave us their best shot in the second half. Everything they threw at us, we had the answer. That answer was Chris Lofton! Chris finished with 34 points to lead us to a 76-58 win. Lofton, once again, proved that he is a prime-time player and there is not a defense in the country that can stop him. After a tough start, I managed to bounce back and finished the game one rebound shy of a double-double with 11 points and nine rebounds. This was a huge victory for our team, fans, and program.

After a huge win, going to The Strip can be exciting. It's almost like a movie. As soon as you walk into a bar or club, everyone starts high-fiving and hugging you. It doesn't matter if they know you or not. At some places, the whole bar may begin cheering and chanting. It is a cool experience for a college athlete.

My parents and older brother went out to celebrate with me. The funniest occurrence of the evening was a friendship that dad made with a college student. My dad's not shy, and will speak his mind to someone criticizing his children. During my freshman year, a college student was sitting behind my parents at a game and made an insulting remark about Dane Bradshaw. My dad had some choice words for him, then my parents found other seats. Tonight, a student comes up to talk to me about the game. He sees my parents and introduces himself to my dad, admitting that he was the kid who aggravated him a few years back. He apologized and my parents burst into laughter. My dad joked with him and gave him a hard time. By the end of the evening, he and my dad are laughing and enjoying each other's company and are best friends.

There may not be a person who wanted to beat the Memphis Tigers more than our assistant coach, Jason Shay. Shay is phenomenal with his opponent scouting skills. Last year, he was assigned to scout Memphis, which was a game we were not supposed to win. But you couldn't tell him that. He knew we were good enough to beat them. This was a game he had been waiting for a year to avenge. Shay deserves much of the credit for our win. He and Coach Pearl designed a beautiful game plan and all we had to do was execute it. Shay has an incredible knowledge of the game and I continue to try to pick his brain to become a more knowledgeable player.

Shay came from humble beginnings. He actually was a walk-on at Iowa while Coach Pearl was an assistant there. He helped coach the freshman team at his high school while working on his masters. He wanted to get into college coaching and interviewed for an assistant position on Pearl's staff at Southern Indiana. Shay was a finalist, but Pearl hired Ken Johnson, who is now our Director of Basketball Operations. Pearl recommended Shay to a friend coaching at Mercyhurst College—a Division II school in Pennsylvania. Shay was hired and spent two years there before learning that Pearl was hiring at University of Wisconsin-Milwaukee. Shay wanted to work for Pearl, but knew that sending in a resume would not be enough. So he called the basketball office, only to get Pearl's voice mail. He left a message, but did not stop there. Shay would spend the next three days calling every hour on the hour from 8 a.m. till 6 p.m. hoping that Coach Pearl would eventually answer his call. Finally, he connected with Pearl, who said he would interview him but Shay needed to be in Milwaukee the next day. At this point, Shay is young, married and broke, plus he is in Pennsylvania, and needs to get to Milwaukee by 9 a.m. the next day. His parents wired him $100 to help make the trip. He made a 10-hour drive through the night and arrived at a nearby town at 3 a.m. where he slept a few hours before his important interview.

Shay was hired, so it was worth the drive, but getting back would be a problem. As he neared the final exit before the Indiana and Ohio state border, he realized he was running out of gas and he didn't have enough money to even pay the toll that was ahead. He pulled over at a rest area and waited for the money his wife, a schoolteacher, sent to the account. Unfortunately, it was about 4 p.m. and the money would not be in the account until after midnight. Shay waited for eight hours for gas and toll money. A few times he impatiently checked to see if the money had been deposited, costing him two dollars that he didn't have with each attempt at the ATM. Eventually, Coach Shay would make it home to Pennsylvania and soon moved to Milwaukee, where he became an important member of Coach Pearl's staff.

December 7-12, University Exams

Exams are the main focus during this time, and we don't have a game until December 16. Coach Pearl realizes the importance of exams and grades, so we have only practiced every other day during this time.

December 16, Western Kentucky Hilltoppers

Western Kentucky is a team that is picked to win their league and be in the NCAA tournament. So while some spectators may not respect Western Kentucky, we realize this will be a tough game and we will have to work to emerge from the game with a win.

Ryan Childress was the most valuable player in the game. He knocked down a three early on and made the plays that win games. The most important play of the game was made when Ryan took a charge on Courtney Lee. Lee was the focus of our scouting report and is expected to be an NBA player. We knew that we needed to get him in foul trouble and we could do that by drawing charges. Ryan drew Lee's second foul on a charge he took at half court. This not only resulted in Lee's second foul, but also prevented a fast-break opportunity for Western Kentucky. No play takes more sacrifice than standing your ground to take a charge and Ryan was able to change the game by doing it. We were able to capitalize with Lee on the bench and never looked back. Chris Lofton continued his amazing hot streak. The +/- chart that we all look at should be renamed "Were-you-in-the-game-with-Chris-Lofton" chart. I am joking but I love it when Chris goes on one of his scoring binges while I'm in the game because I know my +/- is soaring.

December 17-18, Oklahoma State Cowboys

The bus left Thompson-Boling Arena around 10 a.m. on December 17, as we headed to Nashville to face Oklahoma State for a "neutral site" game. We left early because we were given the opportunity to go to a Tennessee Titans' football game before our practice time.

The football game was great and we enjoyed the 70-degree weather in mid-December. The Titans won with some tremendous defensive plays. Soon, our fun was out of the way and we headed to practice.

We are playing at the Gaylord Entertainment Center, which is a great arena for basketball games. Our team played two games there last year and we have already played two games there this year. Our record at Gaylord is three wins and one loss.

Oklahoma State is one of the few undefeated teams left in the country. At 11-0, they are ranked 15th in the country. They also handed us our biggest loss of the season a year ago. They are very physical and pride themselves on their toughness.

Earlier in the week, I met with our team chaplain, James "Mitch" Mitchell, who does a great job with all the athletes. At home games and after our pregame meal, Mitch leads a devotional for the players. Mitch seldom comes on the road with us. Remembering Allan Houston's inspirational devotional, I thought I might do something similar. I talked with Mitch about possibly leading the guys in a devotional when we were on the road. Mitch and I worked on a topic for me to share with the others.

At our pregame meal, I spread the word that after we ate there would be a short devotional for those interested in attending. I felt a little uncomfortable but joked that Brother Dane was going to lead us to the Promised Land. About eight players, who were the usual guys that Mitch leads on game days back in Knoxville, participated. As we closed in prayer, the guys seemed appreciative. This was an opportunity to do something positive. Who knows, maybe I can lead us through devotionals at away games this year and then someone else can do it next year. Then it could become a healthy tradition among UT players. That would be a tradition I would be proud to have helped initiate.

We headed to the gym and everyone seemed focused. Coach had told us earlier that we had an opportunity to separate ourselves from last year's team. The Memphis game was a game we had lost a year ago, but we changed that with this year's team. Oklahoma State was a team that beat us last year, but we can change that with this year's team as well.

The game began and I was able to get into an early rhythm and scored, had a steal, and some assists. Then the referees took me out with two quick touch fouls. An illegal screen and a clean swipe of the ball were called fouls, and I went to the bench.

The game went back and forth and was physical like we expected. We trailed by six at halftime after their big man knocked down a three at the buzzer. We were confident in the locker room, but were annoyed because we felt we should have had the lead. The emphasis of the second half was to put more pressure on them defensively. So many things happened in the course of the second half that it is hard to remember it all.

It seemed like we were always on the verge of taking the lead but they would answer with a basket. So many players made big plays for us. Duke proved himself to be one of the top freshmen in the country; Wayne played huge; Ramar and Jordan continued to impress at the point guard spot and Chris and JaJuan were phenomenal on the perimeter. JaJuan led us with six steals and Chris made several nice shots including a three, plus the foul.

I have to brag about my coaching on the court. Several times I looked at the OSU bench and noticed that Coach Sutton would call a post-up play for whichever big man I was guarding. I would let them set up the play and then quickly yell at Wayne to switch men. As a result, they were posting up against Wayne which is not the advantage they were looking for. I could see the frustration on Coach Sutton's face, combined with the confusion of the player posting up unexpectedly against Wayne. I loved the fact that I was almost coaching against him as a player on the floor…and winning. We tricked them on defense in this way about four or five times in the second half. Wayne, especially, got a kick out of the strategy, laughing and saying, "Dane, you keep tricking 'em."

In the end, it all came down to the final 40 seconds. They dribbled up the court and had an offensive play set up. I recognized the set immediately from the film room (a play they killed us with last year). I ran over the two screens I knew were being set for me and was able to front the post. They had nothing. My man continued to try and post up and they eventually forced it into him because they had no backup plan. I reached around and batted the ball with my right hand as they attempted to pass it into the post. Duke hustled down the loose ball and now we were in a position to win the game.

We had a play designed from the previous time out for this situation. It is play where I come off a screen to the block in hopes for an open layup, but if I am not open I can get the ball and hit Chris, who is circling around the wing for a shot. Well, they took away part of the play and Duke was able to force it into me on the block, but we were somewhat in scramble mode. Ramar was in the corner and he cut baseline yelling my name, "Dane! Dane!" I dished it off to him and he went up with a power layup that came off the rim. And there I was, right place and right time. I jumped up with my right arm extended as I held off the defender with my left. I stretched out my arm and got a tip in basket with 1.9 seconds left. They called time out and I leaped into the air for a chest bump with Duke Crews (Of course, he was a little higher than me on the chest bump). OSU designed an effective play but they missed at the buzzer. It is a good thing too, because the player obviously traveled and, had he made it, I think Coach Pearl would have gone insane. When asked about the tip-in, my truthful response was, "right place, right time." But one thing I've noticed is the harder you work, the luckier you seem to get.

On a side note, Jacqui Pearl, the coach's daughter, sang the national anthem tonight. We are undefeated when she sings, with big wins including tonight, Florida, and Memphis.

The fans were the MVP. This was called a neutral site game, but the Vol fans filled the arena and made it a home atmosphere for us. It was a great advantage. I was called over by the ESPN reporters to do a post-game interview with Coach Pearl. It all happened so fast that I was still in disbelief. I just made a game-winning basket and I am getting interviewed by ESPN on national TV; I was living a dream and didn't have time to react.

I thought it must have been more than a coincidence that I began a Bible study the same day I have something like this happen to me. Jordan joked, "I'm leading devotional next week, if that's the outcome." The greatest feeling to me was that my teammates, who are my extended family, were so happy for me. If you have respect and love from your own locker room then you are graced.

This all seems too familiar, though. I am scheduled for a MRI on my shoulders tomorrow and anxiously await the results. Tomorrow will be a big day for me. As great as tonight was, based on past experience, I know tomorrow could hold an entirely different outcome.

December 19, Another MRI

I woke up after a short night's sleep and drove to the basketball office to pickup the paperwork for my MRI. It was a joyful environment in the office. I was laughing with Coach Pearl about my postgame interview with ESPN, and told him I did my best to help recruit. He said, "I know. The guy asked about the game-winning shot and you just went on talking about how great the coaches were and what a great program it was." We laughed, but, hopefully, I did help influence some bigtime recruits to choose the University of Tennessee.

I met with Chad before going to the hospital. I joked that with as much attention as I was getting about this MRI, they better find something wrong or I'm going to look like a wuss. Of course, I pray there is nothing wrong but I will have some friends make fun of me if it just comes back negative.

I sat in the lobby of the hospital next to an elderly couple. The man was reading the sports section with my picture on the front. The nice lady turned to me and asked, "Did you go to the game last night?" I laughed, inwardly, and answered, "Yes Ma'am. I was there." She continued to ask questions about the game, and I did my best to politely answer her questions. But when she asked, "Did you have good seats?" I had to tell her, "Actually, I was playing in the game. So, I guess you could say I had good seats." She looked confused and asked which player I was. I just pointed at the big picture in the paper right next to her and said, "That one. My name is Dane, nice to meet you."

We laughed and she seemed a little embarrassed but she shouldn't have. It was a humorous coincidence that she asked if I attended the big game, just as her husband held up a picture of me celebrating our team's victory on the cover of the newspaper.

I arrived at the hospital around 10 a.m. and didn't leave until about 2 p.m. I had to be injected in both shoulders with a dye that allows the doctors to better read the results of the MRI. If you have never had an MRI, it is not the most comfortable procedure. I lay flat on the bed and they pushed me into this machine which has no space to move in any direction. This helps you stay completely still. I tried to take a nap but, with all the noise of the machine, it is like trying to sleep in a construction site. You can hear the noises, even while wearing the headphones they provide. I was in the machine for about an hour-and-a-half as I had both shoulders examined. I was told that they would have the results in a couple of hours. All I could do then was wait.

I tried to stay busy and did some Christmas shopping to help keep my mind off potentially bad results. After a couple of hours I received a text message from Chad, saying he wanted to talk to me about the MRI results. I called him right away because the tone of the text sounded like bad news. However, Chad told me that it seemed to be tendinitis in the right shoulder with some inflammation in the rotator cuff. All I could say was, "So there is nothing torn? No surgery or anything like that, right?" He said, "No," and I was one relieved individual. There were so many friends and family praying for me. I was grateful for everyone's concern and I know their prayers helped. Tendinitis and inflammation may not sound like the toughest injury, but I'll take it.

There was more media attention about the MRI than anyone could have imagined. For me, the knowledge that I don't have a serious injury puts my mind at ease and allows me to get on with my activities and life.

December 20-22, Preparation for the Texas Longhorns

We met as a team before we began preparations for the Texas game. Coach congratulated us on the highest team GPA in years. We had a combined 2.9 GPA and nine Vol Scholars. To be a Vol Scholar you must have a 3.0 or above. I finished with three A's and one B in my first semester of grad school, which is the best I have had in a while. At 3.75, I believe I was highest on the team so that should keep my parents happy. Coach Pearl was appreciative, because he realizes there are many programs worrying about the eligibility of their players. There were numerous study hall and tutor hours put into the success of our student-athletes, and we are all especially proud of those who have to work extra hard to achieve success in the classroom. The people who should be congratulated more than anyone are Lauren Mackey, our academic advisor at the Thornton Center, and Ken Johnson who has several academic related duties. It can be a thankless job, but they work exceptionally hard to help the players successfully balance basketball and school.

After practice, I met with the media. I felt like I was Terrell Owens or something. Journalists and radio and television reporters surrounded me to talk about the results of my MRI. I appreciated their concern and was amazed there was so much public interest in the condition of my shoulder. I thought to myself, "If this many people seem to care about my shoulder maybe they will buy a copy of this book I am writing."

It's December 21 and while I received great medical news yesterday, Jordan received the complete opposite today. We had a tough conditioning practice, but only had contact drills for about five minutes. Coach said, "We are only going to play live for five minutes and that's it." Well, with Jordan Howell's luck no time seems to be safe. In the first play of the drill, Jordan got his hand caught in a player's jersey and obviously hurt himself badly. His hand swelled immediately, and we all knew something was wrong because of the hand injury he went through to start the season. After practice, he was X-rayed and they found a break in his right hand. The break was on the same hand he broke previously this season—same injury. We felt awful for him. Talk about snakebit! As soon as this great guy recovers from a broken hand and fights his way into the starting lineup, this happens again. It just seems he can't catch a break. I continue to tell him something great will happen in his favor. It may not happen until his senior season, but sooner or later his work ethic will pay off.

As Jordan went home depressed about the injury, the rest of us went to the mall where we rang bells for the Salvation Army. We were set up at different stations throughout the mall. Wayne and I were partners. We appeared to be taking in some serious cash with many donations filling the pot. The timing couldn't have been better for us to lend our support to a charitable cause. It is Christmas time and we just came off a great win. With this combination, almost everyone was donating. I joked with Wayne, "I'm glad we won our last game. If we had lost this pot might be empty." It was fun for us and it was a good opportunity to speak with some fans while helping raise money for a great organization—the Salvation Army.

December 23, Texas Longhorns

Our team made a grand entrance through the stands, walking up five flights of steps to get to the concourse level. It was a unique way of entering the gym and allowed us to get close to our fans.

This approach generated a lot of positive fan reaction, but, unfortunately, the first half wasn't pretty for the Vols. We were outplayed and found ourselves down by 15 at the half. Because of a bad reaction to medicine for my shoulder I had an IV before the game and received another IV at halftime. I definitely was of little help to the team. As Coach came into the locker room he basically laid out two options: get our ass beat by 35 or fight back, play with some pride, and get a memorable win.

We ran out of the locker room ignited and ready to make a comeback. We quickly cut the lead to 10 and were back in the game. There was little doubt in our minds that this would come down to the wire. Slowly but surely we crawled back into the game. I played limited minutes as the fans got a preview of next year's team. Ramar, Chris, JaJuan, Wayne, and Duke led the charge. Their play was phenomenal. Duke seems to get better each game, and he is responsible for our strong start to the second half. We trailed with the score 85-87. With under a minute remaining, Chris Lofton made what should be known as "The Shot." As the shot clock wound down, Chris pulled up from the left side of the court parallel to the "T" in Tennessee near the midcourt area. He rose up and let the ball fly as future NBA lottery pick Kevin Durant stretched his arm out in an attempt to block the shot. Durant is 6'10" and Chris is 6'2" but there is something special about Chris that can't be explained. The shot seemed to take forever in the air and then it dropped through the net to give us a one point lead. We got a defensive stop but only made one of our free throws after being fouled. Durant made a bucket to send it into overtime.

We dominated overtime by scoring 22 points, but this was all about the shot Lofton made. At this point, we all feel privileged to be playing with the guy because as much as this has become the "Bruce Pearl Era" it is the "Chris Lofton Era," as well. Chris would be the first to admit that he wasn't alone in this game.

Ramar Smith continued to grow as a player with his best game. He had 16 points, nine assists, and zero turnovers. It is amazing how far Ramar has come since the beginning of the season as he becomes more and more comfortable. The coaching staff has to be credited with the development of the young players. Wayne Chism performed great in overtime as he attempted and converted a three-pointer that seemed to have everyone saying, "No!" before he shot it and "Yea Wayne!" after it went through the hoop. Duke, Ramar, and Wayne played huge parts in our victory and it is easy for us to forget they are freshmen. It's a good thing when people forget you are a freshman because that means you are not making the usual novice mistakes.

It's Christmas time and after the game, the Vol players begin to disperse to their homes across the country to celebrate the holiday and to rest. I received a cortisone shot after the game to help relieve my shoulder pain. After my third needle of the day, I was definitely ready to get home and I boarded a flight to Memphis. As I landed and walked through the airport with my bags I realized how different my hometown was from Knoxville, because I'm not recognized nearly as much. Knoxville is wonderful and the University of Tennessee is such an unbelievably great place to be a college athlete. But it was a great feeling to be getting home and being able to lie on my favorite couch and be around family. There would be no basketball, no practice, no reporters; just family and delicious food.

December 26, Back to Basketball

The break away from basketball was short but sweet. After a couple of days off, I think we are all anxious to get back to playing. We felt a renewed sense of motivation heading to the gym because of the time away. The latest Top 25 rankings provided us with some motivation as well. The AP poll ranked us at number 21 but the coaches' poll left us unranked. We have won six straight with a convincing win over Memphis, we beat an undefeated Oklahoma State team, and we just beat Texas. What more do they want? Not to mention, the only games we have lost are to number two North Carolina and number 16 Butler. Technically, we don't have any bad losses and have some great wins, but I guess we still have to gain some respect. Teams like Michigan State were ranked instead of us. I think this has a lot to do with the consistency of the program. Michigan State has proven themselves for several years and we are still proving ourselves as a consistent team. But Coach Pearl's teams have been anything but inconsistent. Rankings aren't that important, but I and many other Vol supporters feel we were a bit disrespected in the recent polls, especially the coaches' poll.

We met as a team before we turned our focus toward Tennessee Tech. One thing Coach Pearl is good at is forward thinking. As good as everything is going for us, he knows that we will have some adversity sooner or later. He asked us how we would have reacted had we lost some of the games we had just won. We need to be prepared to face adversity, so we will be able to react to it in a positive manner.

Our team watched film and listened to the scouting report. The coaching staff prepared for Tennessee Tech with the same urgency as Texas. They watch and study just as much film on a supposedly lesser opponent as they do a Top 10 team. I'm not sure that all coaches do this, but our coaching staff puts 100 percent into everything they do. Our coaches got to Tennessee by upsetting the higher ranked teams when they were working with overlooked underdog teams. So, they know what it is like to be on the other end and they don't intend to have done to them what they were successful in doing to others.

December 28, Tennessee Tech Golden Eagles

It was a tough night for any opponent to come into Thompson-Boling Arena. We had several players set career highs in a number of statistical categories. While Tennessee Tech is a talented team, we were hitting on all cylinders, which made it difficult for them to stay close. JaJuan Smith set a career high with 23 points against a team close to his hometown that did not recruit him. It was nice to see him continue to prove people wrong. Ryan Childress took up most of the room on the player-ticket list as he had about 15 family members drive down for the game. Whenever you play in front of your family there is a little extra pressure. If Ryan had to choose a game to play well in, I believe this one would be near the top of his list. Hard work and self discipline paid off tonight for Ryan. He had a career-high 13 points and 11 rebounds. Ryan gave us some help off the bench his freshman year, but for him to put up 13 points and 11 rebounds far exceeds his play from a year ago. To be able to have a career game in front of his extended family, had to be a highlight of his career. Duke Crews was unhappy with the way he played, yet he had his first career double-double with 10 points and 10 rebounds. I'll take him being unhappy with a double-double any day of the week.

In all the years of the Tennessee basketball program there has never been a triple-double. I will never leave Tennessee as an all-time leader in a specific category, but a goal of mine is to be the first ever to get a triple-double. I flirted with that tonight as I had seven points, tied a career high with nine assists, and seven rebounds. This is the type of game where one is most likely to get a triple-double. I'm not sure how realistic it is to fulfill this dream once we get into SEC play. I probably missed an opportunity, but maybe it will come when I least expect it.

I also had a career high and career first by receiving a technical foul. I deserved it because I got caught talking a little trash to the opponent after I made a move in the lane and scored over a particular defender. The same person I scored on was the one who started the trash talking the play before, but the person who retaliates is usually the one who gets caught. On the previous play, this player felt it necessary to point out the fact that I was a "weak ass white boy." I wish I had a dollar for every time I heard these words throughout my career. In response, I drove it in and scored over him and had a few choice words for him as the ball went through the hoop. Then I heard the whistle blow and knew the referee had caught me. He pointed at me signaling technical foul and for a brief second I acted like I didn't know what he was talking about (like all innocent yet guilty players do). As Coach Pearl argued the call, I came over and had to admit that I had mouthed off. I didn't think Coach would get so upset, given the score of the game and the fact that this never happens to me. However, he just kept on arguing in my defense. I laughed, but it is great to have a coach that has your back.

There were about a thousand kids who attended camp this summer in attendance at tonight's game. We had a table set up to sign autographs for them after the game. We assumed that many of the kids would leave considering it was 9 p.m. and thought that the autograph session would take about fifteen minutes. As we went to our designated area, we saw the tremendous line wrap around the entire arena. This was going to take forever. Many of the players stayed as long as they could and were very courteous to the campers. But when the clock rolled around to 10:30 p.m. only Chris, Tony, and I were still there. We were very tired and still in our sweaty jerseys from the game, but we realized how much this meant to the kids. Our thought process was that if a mother and child waited in line, then the least we could do was stick around and sign a poster. We are lucky that anyone cares to have our autographs. I also thought about when I was these kids' age, and how I would have felt if I had waited in line and a player I admired left before I had a chance to meet him. It took about an hour-and-a-half to sign all the autographs, but we owed it to our young fans that supported us and came to our camp.

December 29, Marques Johnson Leaves the Team

We met as a team in the film room before practice as usual, except there was one player missing. Coach informed us that freshman guard Marques Johnson had decided to transfer and was heading home to Indiana. I was aware of this possibility because Coach Pearl called me over the Christmas break and told me that Marques probably was going to transfer to another school; however, then Coach called the next day, saying that Marques had decided to stay.

His coaches and teammates hated to hear this news about Marques. He is a promising player and is well liked. He was going to redshirt this year, and was unhappy with his situation as a point guard, seeing himself having to play behind Jordan and Ramar next year as well. He wanted immediate playing time and no one can blame him for that because we all want to play. He had his opportunities early in the season, but he just wasn't quite ready for significant playing time.

We understood Marques' decision. But some of us felt that if you aren't receiving enough playing time you bust your butt in the off season and prove yourself to where the coaches can't deny you playing time. Another factor is in college sports anything can happen. Injuries, ineligibility, and disciplinary problems are all possibilities that could happen at any time, opening a door for

Marques. Also, success is much sweeter after fighting through adversity. None of us knock Marques for transferring because he needs to do what is best for him. But as Marques' friend I wish, if he was going to transfer, he would have finished the year out. Who knows where this team could go? Sweet 16? Elite Eight? Who knows? Even as a redshirt, what an incredible experience it would be just to be part of something great with your teammates and friends.

In Coach Pearl's 14 years of coaching, he has never had one of his recruits transfer, so this was a new experience for the coach. I truly wish Marques the best. I just think there were great times ahead for him at the University of Tennessee.

A fallout of Marques' departure was that his locker was now available for someone else's use. Walk-ons share a locker, and now there is an open locker available for one of them. Immediately after practice the walk-ons competed in one-on-one games to see who gets their own locker. It was fun to watch and there were some intense games. Eventually, it was Tanner Wild who was victorious. Tanner didn't seem interested in the one-on-one games, but he took advantage of the situation and moved his gear into the empty locker, because he is the veteran walk-on.

December 30, East Tennessee State University Buccaneers

This is one of my favorite games to play because I have two former high school teammates on the other side. Travis Strong is one of my best friends. Together, we graduated from White Station High School in Memphis and were teammates on state championship teams. We have supported one another throughout our college careers. Unfortunately, Travis tore his ACL early in the year and is receiving a medical redshirt this year. Another close friend and former teammate for ETSU is Courtney Pigram.

Courtney has done extremely well at ETSU, and it is great to see our high school represented well at the college level.

ETSU has not played since December 21. Therefore, they have had plenty of time to prepare for us. They bothered us with a trapping defense we had not seen. Yet we still managed to get an 18-point lead. They never gave up and all of a sudden we had blown the lead and were in a tight game. We began playing out of character and panicked a bit, but Chris and JaJuan made huge plays for us to come out victorious. The final score was 93 to 88. ETSU is a good team, but this really could have been one of those losses that would have haunted us with the NCAA Selection Committee. Somehow we've got to learn how to finish a team off once we get a large lead.

We all know what Chris is going to bring to the table, but JaJuan is having a great junior season thus far. For the second game in a row, he has scored 23 points. Perhaps more important than his offense, is the energy he brings to the team. He sets the tone on defense, as well as the tone in our press, and he has become a heck of an offensive weapon on the perimeter. Here is a guy who was lightly recruited and came to UT as a walk-on. A scholarship opened up almost as soon as he got to campus and it became his. JaJuan is a fierce competitor and when he brings his intensity the whole team benefits. He is overshadowed due to Chris' greatness, but he has combined with Chris to become one of the most feared backcourts in the SEC.

After a poor team outing, we were anxious to see Coach Pearl's reaction. Before the game, he had planned to give us the next two days off. We all sat nervously, waiting to see if he would change his mind due to our play. He got fired up for a while, but with 12 wins he reminded us what a great year 2006 has been and that we should be thankful for our blessings. Finally, he said what we all wanted to hear, "We will take the next two days off."

January 3, Reflections on 2006

Other than Ohio State on January 13, we have finished nonconference play. I skimmed through my journal notes, and couldn't help but reflect on the amazing number of ups-and-downs that our team and we as individuals have gone through in just one half of the season. We've lost a couple of important players, we went to New York and lost an important opportunity to showcase our team by promptly losing two games, and we have been beset with some major injuries. Yet, we have hung together as a team and already have tasted sweet victory 12 times.

Philosophically, I guess one of our lessons to be learned or at least reinforced is to not allow our lows to be too low or our highs to be too high. As Coach says, "Focus on the process, not the end result." It is such a long season and there are more victories and defeats to come. A great thing about our sport of basketball is that by playing approximately 30 games, a team like ours has the opportunity to share many positive experiences.

As a team, we have done a great job of picking up the slack if one player is not playing particularly well one night. I just hope our best play is ahead of us. It had better be as the start of our SEC competition is only a few days away.

January 7, Mississippi State Bulldogs

Conference play is without question the most important part of the season. We open up at home against Mississippi State with an opportunity to start 1-0 in conference play. They are a young team that we handled easily a year ago in Starkville, but they are a much improved team. The star of their team is Tennessee native Jamont Gordon. Jamont and I became friends as I hosted him on official and unofficial visits to UT during the recruiting process. I suspect few people realize how much player-to-player networking and attempts to aid the recruiting process go on behind the scenes. Jamont seemed to be on his way to UT before Coach Buzz Peterson was fired. Because the people who recruited him were now gone, this caused Jamont to change his mind.

These are the games that we can't afford to lose. It is a home game against a talented team but one that we are capable of beating. Every win in the SEC is important and they all count the same in the won-lost column.

Our style of play can result in huge runs for us. Due to the pace of the game, it can also result in runs for the other team. Today's game was an example, as we traded runs and exchanged punches. We were down by four at one point in the second half but never panicked. No matter the score we always feel like we are going to win the game. We may be down, but we never doubt that we will find a way to win. Duke Crews played like a man in his SEC debut with 18 points. Chris gave us 11 of his 21 points in the last five minutes. It is great to have a weapon like Chris when you can just give the ball to him in a close game and know he is almost automatic from the free throw line. We came out with a 92 to 84 win despite a 25-point, 11-rebound, nine-assist performance from Jamont Gordon.

One thing we stress before every game is defense and rebounds. It is always written at the top of the drawing board in the locker room; "Defense and rebounding wins championships." With that said, our defense and rebounding was nonexistent. Offensively we are fine but we can't just depend on outscoring opponents to win. I know that approach will catch up with us sooner or later, just as it did a year ago. In a tournament setting, it eventually comes down to the better defensive team. We realize that we will give up a number of points because of our style, but the shooting percentages and rebounding margins are statistics that we should have a measure of control over. Coach was upset and I knew it was going to be ugly in the film room the next day. However, a win is a win and we are fortunate to be 1-0, but we know we must get better defensively to be a special team.

January 8, Learning Defense

One of the most dreaded events as a college basketball player on Coach Bruce Pearl's teams is practice day after a terrible defensive performance. It's not the on-court practice that we dread so much. It's the film room. We all hoped we would just move on to Vanderbilt, but instead we had to watch the first half of the Mississippi State game to try and learn from our mistakes. We sat in the dark, stadium film room as the projector came down from the ceiling. We all knew it was going to get uncomfortable as Coach pressed play. One of the most nerve-wracking, anxious feelings is sitting in a dark room beside Coach Pearl as you witness visual evidence of defensive mistakes and lack of effort. The worst is when you know your mistake is coming up on film and all you can do is sit and wish that somehow Coach accidentally hits the fast forward button.

Each error on the court continues to add fuel to the fire and the frustration builds in Coach's voice. I sit next to him and after bad games, it's like sitting through a horror movie. His face gets more-and-more red, and sometimes his spit splashes on my arm. He has a remote laser pointer. He uses this with its red dot visual to point out exactly what the problem is and who is screwing up. Each time that red dot is pointed in your direction on film, you are probably the one who messed the play up. It is like a video game to see how many times Coach assassinates you with the laser gun. You just try to survive from one play to the next.

These film sessions aren't meant to strike fear in us or just subject us to criticism, rather the aim is to teach and make us aware of the mistakes we are making on the floor. Right now, the mistakes we are making will not allow us to be a great team. What

Coach tries to do is make us learn from this after a win rather than learn from a loss. Defense and rebounding wins championships and we did neither last game. It can take up to an hour to watch 10 minutes of game film with Coach Pearl, depending on how much detail he wants to cover. By the end of this session, Coach *slams* the remote down and simply said, "I can't watch this anymore. Get out to the court." And Coach wonders why the remote doesn't work sometimes.

January 9, Academics

School starts this week so we had a few academic housekeeping items to cover. Our basketball team is split into three different academic teams for the semester. Your team is awarded points based on study hall appointments, extra tutor sessions, grades, etc. I captained my team to victory this semester as Tanner, Justin, Wayne, JaJuan, and I defeated the other two teams. We were awarded a nice fleece jacket with a Vol scholar patch on it.

Coach Pearl emphasizes the importance of school. He knows that his players thrive on competition and found this was a good way to jack us up with our school work. We actually get into this academic competition. Guys are always trying to get extra points for their respective teams. We had a number of players earning GPAs over 3.0. We will have the same competition this next semester, so we'll see if our fivesome can repeat as academic champs.

January 10, Vanderbilt Commodores

Basketball bragging rights across the state of Tennessee are great to have. We have wins over ETSU, Tennessee Tech, and Memphis. If we can take care of Vanderbilt both times we play them we could sweep the state of Tennessee. More important, it would be a road win we need in conference play.

Vanderbilt's court is unique. It is a raised floor with fans and commentators on either side of the court at "foot level." The benches are underneath each basket so communication is always tough when you can't see the bench for play calls, etc. We can't even hear Coach Pearl when this place gets loud.

Regardless of records, talent, or environment the UT-Vandy game is usually hard fought and often goes down to the wire before the winner is determined. It was no different tonight with a sellout crowd on hand.

We went into the locker room at halftime after Chris Lofton hit the deepest jump shot I have ever seen in person. To put it in perspective, it was far deeper than his Texas shot that I talked about earlier. Chris was about a foot in front of half court when he calmly rose up and shot a regular jump shot. He had the opportunity to get closer to the basket as the clock wound down, but he knew he could make it from where he was standing which is unbelievable. He put us in a good position to win the game. Vandy made a high percentage of their shots but we held them to only one offensive rebound.

The second half was a different story. They beat us to loose balls, they were the aggressor and they dominated the glass with 11 offensive rebounds. The final offensive rebound was by Shan Foster on a tip in at the buzzer. It was fitting that we lost on an offensive rebound because that's what we deserved. Their game-winning shot followed a beautiful pick and roll by Ramar and Duke as Duke finished with a two-handed dunk on what seemed to be the game-winning basket.

But everything Coach had warned us about caught up to us. You can only survive so long when you don't consistently defend and rebound. Our locker room, which was more of a broom closet (thanks Vandy), was deadly silent. We all sat there numb with shock. Coach found a way to tell us we didn't deserve to win, without crushing our spirits. I deserved much of the blame, making some defensive slipups toward the end of the game. For me, this is worse than missing shots. To be a winning team your veterans just can't do this.

Duke could have been the hero but because we couldn't finish with a defensive stop, his play will soon be forgotten. It is a sickening feeling. You know your team will lose at some point, but losing at the buzzer just takes the breath out of you, even though it's part of the game. We can't have them all go our way and good things have to happen to other people as well.

The Vanderbilt players were ecstatic and deserved a win of this magnitude. I just hate that it came at our expense. A guy like Dan Cage, whose role for his team is similar to mine, is a hard working, deserving senior who will never forget the night he helped beat the Tennessee Volunteers. Derrick Byars is a lifelong friend of mine from Memphis. He is another guy that I played with for years and against in high school. Byars had 25 points and led his team to victory.

January 11, The Fruits of Defeat

It is tough walking on campus the day after a loss, especially to Vanderbilt. Most everyone come across either asks about the game, apologizes about the loss or says nothing. You can tell they are thinking about last night's loss, just as you are. It's embarrassing to have so many others sharing the same sour mood you helped create.

I hope all my teammates realize this and we can improve as we shift gears to play Ohio State University.

January 12, Team Nicknames

We are on the plane to Columbus, Ohio, right now to face the number five team in the country on their home court. With little else to do on the plane, I whipped out the laptop and worked on my journal. I have been meaning to make a journal entry, sharing our team nicknames. I wanted to preserve these names for posterity, especially since some of the guys are embarrassed by their use. Our team roster and respective nicknames follow:

JaJuan Smith — alias "Juan" or "Lil' Town" because he comes from the small town of Cleveland, Tennessee.

Chris Lofton — alias "C-Lo" or "Franklin" which is his middle name he is embarrassed by. I am not sure he would enjoy the crowd chanting "Franklin." If they do in the future, he can blame it on me.

Quinn Cannington — alias "Q."

Justin Jackson — alias "J.J."

Tony Passley — alias "T Pass."

Ramar Smith — alias "Ro," not really sure where the "o" comes in but he has gone by that his whole life.

Steven Pearl — alias "Pearl." Even his dad calls him by his last name.

Tanner Wild — alias "T Wild" or "The Professa," because he resembles the player off the AND1 team.

Rick Daniels Mullhollands — alias "RDM."

Josh Tabb — alias "Tabloid" or "Pops," because he has old man aches and pains all the time. He has the body of a 45-year old.

Dane Bradshaw — alias "DB" or "D Bizzle" jokingly.

Jordan Howell — alias "J Howell" or "JoHo."

Ben Bosse — alias "Big Ben."

Wayne Chism — alias "Weezy."

Duke Crews — just the crowd yelling "DUUUKKKEEEE!" (which I predicted correctly earlier in the book).

Ryan Childress — alias "Chill" or "Chilly."

January 13, Ohio State Buckeyes

What an unbelievable opportunity to bounce back from the Vanderbilt loss and prove ourselves as a successful program. We get to play the number five team in the country on their home floor on CBS. Their team has a number of future draft picks but none more recognizable than freshman phenom Greg Oden. Oden will most likely be the number one or two pick in next year's NBA draft as a skilled, athletic seven-foot true center. Oden is still wearing a brace on his right wrist after a preseason wrist surgery. It was the same surgery that I had on my wrist. The only difference was that mine wasn't updated and reported weekly on ESPN. He is shooting free throws with his left hand because of the injury, and his left has been very effective for him. Actually, it hurts my pride quite a bit because he is shooting free throws with his left hand a hell of a lot better than I'm shooting with my right.

We shot around at the gym in the morning, but came back to the hotel for our walk through. As reported earlier, Coach Pearl never goes over any of our plays or the scout on any court other than our own. He is almost paranoid of a camera lurking somewhere in the arena recording our practice time or an onlooker taking notes. So, we find a large meeting room in the hotel and the managers put tape on the carpet representing half of a court with a free throw lane, three point line, etc. Sometimes they really get into it and decorate the tape setup with a fancy SEC logo in the middle of the lane. We walk through our plays and go over the opponent's plays to review. My guess is our hotel walk through would be entertaining to some outsiders.

Because we are the clear underdog, many are calling this an opportunity game, meaning it would be nice to win but it won't hurt us if we lose. However, this is not our team or staff mindset. We may lose, but we plan and believe we will win every game we play. Of course this is an opportunity to gain respect around the college basketball world. With all the supposed talent on the other team, Coach has emphasized taking pride in our individual match up; this must be done within the framework of the team. Coach Pearl used the nationally televised game as motivation as well. His words were loud and clear, "This game isn't about you. It's about Ohio State. CBS is for North Carolina, Kentucky, Florida, and those types of teams. Not you all. Not me. Not Coach Jones. Make the world respect you the way they do those teams. Today is when you get that respect." With that said, we took the court.

We battled back and forth through the first half though it was dominated by Greg Oden. One of the reasons Coach Pearl originally scheduled this game was for Major Wingate to match up with Greg Oden so Major could get the exposure of NBA scouts. Obviously, we missed Major. Regardless of Oden's performance, we had our Tennessee swagger, confidence and focus that I hadn't seen in a while. It just seemed like we were on our way to a huge upset. The game went back and forth in the second half as we were able to contain Oden more effectively. It was intense throughout and we took the lead after I got a steal by swiping the ball from

Oden with Chris finishing on the other end. With a one-point lead we got the ball in Chris' hands and they were forced to foul him with about 15 seconds to play. Chris is about an 85 percent free throw shooter, but this time the percentages weren't on our side as he missed the front end of a one-and-one. Ohio State set a screen at the top of the key for Ron Lewis and he nailed a three. Lewis only had two points up to that point, but he made the shot when it mattered. I quickly got the ball out of the net and kicked it ahead to Ramar who raced down the court as the clock ticked down. He drove strongly to the basket and put the ball off the glass but it bounced off the rim. There was still hope as Wayne tipped the ball toward the basket, but it, too, bounced off. An Ohio State player chased the ball before it went out of bounds as the clock hit zero. Replays showed the player stepped out of bounds with 1.7 seconds left, but the referee didn't call it. Bottom line, we lost and our competitive hearts were broken. I could barely gather myself to shake hands in line with the opponent as I looked at the scoreboard in disbelief. We had it in our hands and were unable to get the win. Head Coach Thad Matta had some very kind words after the defeat, but nothing could make me feel better at this point.

The locker room was not as silent as the one in Vanderbilt after our loss there. Still, a few players shed some tears after this one. We left everything on the floor and it hurts so much when that results in defeat. This is one of our tougher losses.

No one was harder on themselves than Chris Lofton. He doesn't care that he was the main reason that we were in the game or the fact that, in critical situations, he has bailed us out time and time again. Chris only cares that he missed a free throw at a critical time. All this proves is that he is human, and can sometimes miss just like everyone else. There wasn't much anyone could say to Chris that could cheer him up, but, like just like our wins, we were all in this loss together.

January 14, There was a Sunrise

None of us felt any better but the sun did come up today. One of the hardest things to do is to put a loss behind you and shift your focus to your next opponent. No team in the Southeastern Conference feels sorry for you. Auburn sure isn't feeling sorry for us. They would love to hand us another defeat.

January 17, Auburn Tigers

The whole trip was a nightmare. We took a short flight into Columbus, Georgia, then it took about an hour to drive to the hotel. From the hotel to the arena, it took another thirty minutes. The traveling made everyone tired and cranky, but the worst was yet to come.

Long story short, because I don't even want to talk about it, we blew a 14-point lead and lost. With all due respect to Auburn, I feel we are a better team and we gave this one away. We didn't play to our potential and we lost this game, after we had it in our hands. It was sickening to watch a team celebrate with their fans and celebrate a victory that should have been ours. Hats off to them; they never quit and it led to a win.

The long trip to Alabama was bad, but it was even worse heading home with the smell of defeat permeating the air. When we boarded the bus, SportsCenter was being played on the television, and, as if we needed a reminder, our losing score scrolled across the bottom of the screen. We left the state of Alabama, knowing it was time to get back to Knoxville and get ourselves a win in front of *our fans*.

January 18, Record String of Losses for Coach Pearl

Last night's loss led to Coach Pearl's first three-game losing streak of his head coaching career, which is an amazing streak for someone who has been coaching for almost 15 years. The fact that gnawed at all our psyches was that we could have and probably should have won all three of these games. "Close but no cigar" is an old standard phrase that applied to each game. Even with the bitter taste of defeat fresh in my mouth, I still chuckled inwardly and thought, "A lot of people refer to me as a winner, but I have been a player who during his college career did my part to help one coaching staff get fired and help another coach to set his longest losing streak." *The bottom line is that we need a win!*

January 19, Fox Sports

Coach Pearl has agreed to let Fox Sports "mic" him up and follow him around for the next couple days. Coach made us aware of this and felt that it was a good opportunity to get the program a little exposure. He often has these sort of requests but turns most of them down. He doesn't want promotion of the team to seem like it is about him or become a distraction, but he felt this was going to be good for our basketball program. As I said earlier, Coach Pearl doesn't change one bit when a microphone is around him. With Coach, what you see is what you get. And this approach gains him the respect of most of his associates.

January 20, South Carolina Gamecocks

South Carolina is a team that is down this year and we were able to benefit from that by getting a win. Even though we won, it didn't seem like we had gotten back on track. We played very well in the first half and there were some positives, but we let another large lead slip away and sloppily won the game by three points. We achieved victory but we suffered a devastating loss to our star player. Chris Lofton turned his ankle early in the second half. Everyone held their breath while he was carried off the court.

I played reasonably well but didn't score a point, going zero for four from the field. I had 13 family and friends that had come to town for the game and it was tough having to come out and hug everyone when I was so down on myself, but it's not their fault I miss shots. The great thing is these are the people who love and care about you no matter how you play the game of basketball. As down as I was, particularly about Chris' condition, the best remedy was being around my family and lifelong friends.

January 21, Go Lady Vols

The story of the day and the headline story for every sports channel is that Bruce Pearl painted his chest for the Lady Vols game. By now nothing he does is really a surprise. Coach, along with Steven, Wayne, Josh, Ryan, and Mark Pancratz, had "GO VOLS" spelled out as each person had a letter on his chest. Mark is our Graduate Assistant who has some unusual work assignments. If Coach Pearl tells you to paint your chest orange; you paint your chest orange. One day, when Mark is a head coach, I'm sure he will save the tape of this event as motivation for his graduate assistants. Anyway, they marched down through the student section and had the crowd pumped up. I could only sit and laugh as I watched the game on television from my apartment. Jordan Howell eventually stepped in for Coach Pearl as Coach showered up midway through the first half.

Most everyone loved it and the fans embraced it as they do just about anything Coach does. Of course, there are always some critics. Some negative announcers felt it was unprofessional and that it took away from the game. Those critics obviously take

themselves too seriously. If anyone thinks Coach Pearl is trying to
get his face on camera for personal promotion purposes then they
should check his track record. This guy has been standing on lunch
tables and doing extraordinary antics to promote his basketball
programs long before any media or cameras gave a damn who he
was. Mike Hamilton was okay with it and Pat Summitt (the coach
who has more wins than anyone else in the history of NCAA
Division I basketball, and she is still chalking them up) was all for
it. So what's the problem? Overall, the sports world supported
what Coach Pearl did. His players loved it! **Go Lady Vols!**

January 22, Mr. Chris Lofton

Because Chris Lofton is such a close friend and I know him
so well, I forget what a big deal he is. It is amazing how many
questions I get about Chris' ankle. Everywhere I go, "How's
Chris?" is a reminder of how popular and great a player he is. I see
him every day and forget that he is an All American. Like me, all
of his teammates just don't see him that way, which is a great
compliment to him. There has never been a more humble superstar
player. You would think he would walk around with at least a little
bit of swagger, but he will score 30 points and after the game he is
just ole Chris from Maysville, Kentucky.

Chris is quiet around strangers, but once you get to know
him, and he is comfortable around you, he can be as talkative as
anyone on our team. He is one of us. If you didn't know anything
about our team and saw us together, you probably wouldn't pick
out Chris Lofton as the superstar player. One, he just doesn't look
like a superstar. Two, he is this young guy who laughs at just about
any joke and makes you retell funny stories over and over again.
He is hilarious company and his true humbleness is something we
all recognize and appreciate. Chris was not heavily recruited out of
high school. Many people don't realize that Chris took recruiting

visits to Arkansas-Little Rock and Valparaiso. No offense to those schools, but All-American Chris Lofton was visiting these schools?

Chris is a huge fan of the NBA, and I think being a fan himself helps him realize his influence and importance to his own fans. Chris never turns down an autograph request from a fan and if he comes off as reserved and quiet, that's just who he is. But don't think he doesn't appreciate his friends and fans.

Someday I want to go back to Maysville with Chris just to see what it's like to be a superstar celebrity from such a small town. The impression Chris has given us of Maysville is it's a place where everyone knows everyone else. Chris comes back to Knoxville bragging about facts like *Maysville just got an Applebee's*. Some of us get a little praise when we go back to our respective hometowns, but I guarantee no one receives praise like Chris in Maysville. They even made T-shirts that read, "I'm from Loftonville, Kentucky." Chris single-handedly forced die-hard Kentucky Wildcat fans to cheer for their SEC rival and archenemy —the Tennessee Vols.

Chris is very proud of his roots and where he is from. He gets this from his parents who are unbelievably supportive people. Even though their son is the star, they are all about the team and this is reflected through Chris.

With all this said, it brings me back to the reality of his ankle injury and that it will be impossible to replace him for our next game. His coaches, teammates and fans realize how valuable Chris is to our team. Some fans feel that we can't win a game without Chris in the lineup. They may be right, but the rest of his teammates have to take this as a challenge and prove the doubters wrong.

January 24, Mississippi Rebels

Almost everyone is asleep on the plane as we are set to arrive back in Knoxville around 2 a.m. I can't even think about sleeping. We lost another game on the road tonight and I don't know how many times I have mentioned "blown leads" or not giving the "knockout blow," but it happened again. We played a first half to be proud of and had a 10-point lead with the final 20 minutes left to play. Another slow second-half start haunted us as the lead quickly disappeared. Before we knew it, the final buzzer sounded with the score 83-69. We were outscored by 24 points in the second half as they shot 60 percent. The final score isn't indicative of how close the game was but the bottom line is that we lost and we are 2-3 in SEC play.

With or without Chris, we've repeatedly lost games by surrendering leads. How do we fix it? Are we not as well conditioned as we thought? Are we not mentally tough enough? It is too easy to blame it on youth. But we simply don't defend in the second half and we aren't as aggressive as we seem to be in the first half of the game. We make mental mistakes offensively and defensively which lead to easy baskets for the opponents. This creates a domino effect where swings in confidence and crowd involvement work against us. That means we must absolutely take no possessions off on defense and find a way to put it all together for forty minutes. Teams are going to make shots, runs and make big plays, but we have to control what we can control. As Coach Pearl says, "They are going to make plays, but we can't afford to *give them* any plays."

Basketball isn't fun right now. People often say, "Just go out there and have fun," but the truth is that as a competitor, the best way to have fun is to win. Winning isn't everything and it is easier to find a way to deal with a loss when you feel you have done all you can do, but it's tough for our team to accept losses.

For us, it is not about a loss. It is about losing four out of our last five games and being 2-3 in the SEC.

Hopefully, our best is yet to come. We must continue to believe in what we do, remain positive, try to learn what has put us in this hole and do everything we can to prepare for each opponent. At one time I felt like we were ahead of the pack in the race to the NCAA tournament, but now we are in the mix with everyone else and it can go either way. We have 11 games left in regular season play and these games will determine whether or not we will have the opportunity to have a memorable late run or a season to forget.

January 25, My Little Motivational Talk

Today we had an opportunity to get a nice lift in the weight room. For practice, we only planned to get a good stretch and shoot some free throws. Coach would have liked to kill us but he knew that we needed to physically recover in order to have a productive practice tomorrow in preparation for Kentucky.

We did watch film and Coach spoke to us. When he finished, he asked if anyone else had something to say. This was a setup for me, because as the team captain and sole senior on the squad, I had planned to ask if I could talk to my teammates. I had so many thoughts on my mind about our recent losses that I felt I needed to share them with the team. So many times you think about what you want to say, but you don't stand up and say it. This time I intended to speak my mind. So, I pulled up a stool and faced the team and coaches. I can't remember exactly what I said, but the gist of it was "Guys, this is my last year and my last chance to be a part of an outstanding team. Put yourself in my shoes and you would want your younger teammates to perform to their maximum potential. But, this isn't about me or Kentucky coming up; it's about us and the rest of this season. Please try to play like this is your last year, your last chance; don't wait until your senior year to do it. I don't question how bad any of us want to win, but if we all can start giving a little extra effort whether it's getting a few extra shots after practice, some extra film sessions with the coaches, or extra weights it could benefit us. I think if we all can have a little more urgency to what we do maybe we can get over this hump. The SEC is too good this year for us to hold anything back. Some of you have the opportunity to go the NBA which is an ultimate dream, but college basketball is the last time where the team is a family. We go through everything together, including all the hours of study hall, waking up at 6 a.m. for weights. After college basketball, it will never be the same. Treat my senior year like you would treat your own and want others to treat it. I love ya'll, but I want to win with ya'll too. And that's my little motivational speech."

I had thought about what I was going to say, but I choked up a bit. This caught me off guard. I believe my teammates recognized the emotion, and perhaps it helped them understand that my words were heartfelt and caught their attention. I'm not sure if my talk accomplished anything, except to get some thoughts off my chest. Of course we all know it's going to take a lot more than words to get us wins in the SEC.

January 26, Getting Ready for Kentucky

I would like to say that my little speech was beneficial, but as practice was sloppy and a couple of guys just weren't with it mentally, it was obvious that the speech had not helped. It's hard to comprehend how a person can come to practice and not give his best effort. The whole team suffers when that happens. So sorry for the inconvenience buddy, but there are 14 other players and a coaching staff that are trying to get better, yet you are dogging it. This is like a slap in the face to your teammates. We have lost four out of five and will be playing in Rupp Arena and you aren't motivated to work. Eventually, that attitude led to other players' tempers flaring which in turn caused Coach Pearl to put us on the end line to run sprints. We huddled up as a team, but it isn't about rallying speeches anymore. Either you want to be a part of the solution or the problem. If you're not here to win then take your butt somewhere else. There was a lot of emotion on the court today.

After all this, we started responding as a team and ended the practice sharply. Hopefully, the way we practiced toward the end will have some carryover and we can take that momentum to Lexington. I walked behind Coach Jones, Coach Shay, and Coach Forbes and sarcastically said, "Well, that speech I gave really helped." Coach Forbes quickly responded, as expected, with a smart remark, "Yeah, nice speech Bradshaw. You really turned our season around."

January 27-28, Kentucky Wildcats

As we head to Lexington to take on Kentucky, we know they are 4-2 in league play we are 2-3. So, there is a lot of pressure on us to win. We just hope we want it more than they do and come out victorious.

Some places are highly hyped, yet the arenas do not live up to their billing. That isn't the case with Rupp Arena. The tradition and history speak volumes. In addition, the arena and fans are phenomenal.

Winning at Kentucky is a wonderful feeling. We were able to experience this last year, but a win this year could be just the thing we need to get our season going back in the right direction.

Another good first half. Another bad second half. Another loss. Lack of consistent play for 40 minutes caught up to us again as we allowed another opponent to have a huge second half run. Nobody can really figure out why this is happening. We emphasize practice, and prepare for second-half execution when fatigue is a factor, yet we still have these considerable lapses that we never recover from.

Personally, I was a non-factor and really did nothing special to help our team win. I was just out there running up and down the court with no effectiveness. When we are playing without Chris we can't afford to have other guys have off games. We need a couple of players to have big nights and the rest of the players need to be solid and productive. Well, today I gave us nothing. I don't know what it is about Kentucky, whether it's their one-on-one defense or help defense on penetration, but they have scouted me as well as any opponent in my four years. After multiple attempts, I have yet to have what could be called a "good game" against Kentucky.

We are going through the toughest time since Coach Pearl has been in Knoxville and I, the senior veteran, did nothing to help us get out of the slump. After my effort I wondered if I had begun to lose credibility as a team leader. The only thing I know to do is to keep fighting, and show the character needed to get through these unhappy times.

January 28-30, Georgia on Our Minds

If you thought Coach Pearl was going to let us sit around and feel sorry for ourselves, think again. We arrived back in Knoxville about 7 p.m. but to our surprise we were told to report to the study hall at 7:30 p.m. Can you imagine playing against Kentucky, taking another tough loss, riding back on a bus for three hours, and then being told to go to study hall? That's a behind-the-scenes look at a student-athlete. We have missed a number of days from class due to road games, and that has helped cause a difficult start to the semester. Coach wasn't sending guys to the study hall for punishment, but because he knew there was an opportunity to get caught up on school work. This illustrates Coach's emphasis on academics. On top of that, we were told to be ready for weights at 6:30 a.m. tomorrow.

Everyone arrived on time and ready to work this morning in the weight room. Getting back to work quickly, both academically and physically, showed that we weren't packing it in and were doing everything it took to get back on the winning track.

As we met in the film room, Coach Pearl put it plain and simple, "We need to win six out of our next 10 games. That's the fact and with our program we should be able to do that but it starts Wednesday with Georgia." He called Georgia a must-win game. We didn't look at yesterday's game film as we wanted to look forward and turn all our attention toward Georgia. We seemed to have a much more business-like approach at practice today. I know there are too many dark entries in my journal, and I am sick of making them.

It's January 30 and Coach Forbes is assigned as the Georgia scout; there is no one who wants to get us back on a winning track more than he. Forbes left a rising Texas A&M program as an assistant to become an assistant under Coach Pearl. At this point in the season, Tennessee is unranked and we have lost five out of six games while Texas A&M is ranked sixth in the nation and playing as well as anyone. Forbes will jokingly mumble as we pass one another, "Should have kept my ass at A&M where there were some real players." He brings a defensive mentality from a Texas A&M program where they would grind out victories, usually in low scoring affairs. He admits there is no right way to play the game. Last year while he was there they beat Texas 65-60 and this year we beat Texas 111-105, so there is more than one way to win. Forbes is quite a character. I remember one practice, after we had played poor defense the night before, Coach Pearl teased him saying, "I thought you came here to bring defense." Forbes cleverly responded, "Well, if you'd slow down your damn offense maybe I could." He had the whole gym laughing on that comeback. Forbes is known for adding another nickname for Chris, "Buckeye," in memory of Chris' missed free throw toward the end of the game against the Ohio State Buckeyes. Any of us can be victims of Coach Forbes' jokes.

Adding Steve Forbes to the staff was a great hire by Coach Pearl. Coach Forbes is extremely dedicated, hard working, and has been around the game long enough to know as much as anybody. There are times when you can just tell he hasn't really slept in days. Recruiting, scouting and traveling can take so much out of a person especially when you incorporate the work ethic of Coach Forbes. There just aren't enough hours in the day for this guy. Coach Pearl has worked hard to develop an identity for his staff and teams. Forbes represents and fits in with that identity. It all goes back to our team motto, "Deserve Victory." Coach Forbes, like the rest of the coaches, will outwork you and they deserve victories.

There was an opening in the staff for Coach Forbes, because former assistant Scott Edgar took the head coaching job at Southeast Missouri State (SEMO). Replacing Coach Edgar was not an easy task which is why it took a long time for Coach Pearl to make a decision. Coach Edgar and Forbes share many of the same qualities; old school, hard-nosed, no B.S., workaholics, experienced, and well connected throughout the years. Also, neither one was scared to shoot it to you straight. After we played poorly, Coach Edgar would say, "You guys are stealing from the university. Flat out stealin' money." At first we didn't know what he was talking about until he explained, "You're stealing from the university because you suck and shouldn't be on scholarship; you don't deserve free books."

As seen, both Coach Edgar and Coach Forbes have the personality to make their players want to work, while keeping us relaxed with their humor. Above all, they are both winners and great people. The team became very close with Coach Edgar and I hated to see him leave. He was a big part of helping to turn around the Tennessee basketball program. Every night, I check the scoreboard to see how SEMO did in their game. I have become the biggest SEMO fan in Knoxville. While we all miss Edgar, it is fun to keep track of his progress as a coach. Edgar is our man and I know he will bring success to the SEMO program.

January 31, Georgia Bulldogs

At the end of practice yesterday Coach Pearl put it simply, "Who wants to go to the NCAA tournament more? Us or Georgia?" The message was clear and each of us realized the importance of the game.

We won with a number of players stepping up big. JaJuan continued to pickup the scoring during Chris's absence. Ramar, Duke, and Jordan all had big nights. The happiest individual was Jordan. By now, you know how much this guy has gone through and how hard he works. Tonight he had a career-high 11 points, knocking down three key three-pointers as he got to play his natural position as a shooting guard. Jordan still has his hand taped. He is taping it for protection, but more importantly because the X-rays show that it is still broken. Not many players, especially with a broken hand, can play shooting guard better than Jordan. We were all happy for him. We are also happy that we've learned we could get a quality win against a SEC opponent without Chris in the lineup. It was also important that we were able to hold onto our lead. Speaking of Chris, his ankle is mending and we hope to see him on the floor, even if it's limited action, in our next game against the Florida Gators. We need our All-American back for our home stretch run.

February 2-3, Florida Gators

We travel to Gainesville today, February 2, to play the Florida Gators tomorrow afternoon. This seems like it would be dead man's land but we have won two out of my three visits to The Swamp. The Florida and Tennessee basketball rivalry was not taken seriously until last year. We defeated them in Knoxville and then again at their place. Both games were won in the closing seconds, and both times I was fortunate enough to have the game winning layup. As a result, some have tagged me with the nickname "Gator Killer." There was a lot more involved in those wins than my layups but I like the label. With last year's victory in The Swamp, we officially swept Florida (the eventual national champion) and we were officially crowned as SEC East champs. Florida may have been national champions, but they didn't beat us.

I seem to be a popular player for opposing student sections to heckle, but no one gets after me more than the University of Florida student section. It all started my sophomore year. As I was walking out of the tunnel for warmups I hear, "There's Bradshaw. There he is." I thought, "What the hell do they want from me? I'm averaging about two points a game. Why are they worrying about me?" As I walked onto the court I started hearing chants of what I thought were, "Brittany's Better," and the students had pictures of a pretty blonde. At the time, Brittany Jackson was a popular, attractive Lady Vol and I assumed they were just telling me that a Lady Vol was better than me. However, as we got closer a teammate said, "Ain't that a picture of your sister?" Sure enough it was and they were chanting "Bridget's Better." My sister Bridget had played college basketball at Barry University, a Division II school in Miami. Well, Bridget is also an attractive blonde and it was an old photo from her college days that they had made copies of and passed throughout the student section.

I have no idea who discovered Bridget's old media guide photo and planned this heckling, but I have to give them credit for originality. I couldn't wait to tell my sister her picture had been blown up and was in the hands of the Florida students at the game. In fact, one student, who weighed about 300 pounds, had her picture pinned to his shirt. He was shaking his big fat belly to the music while her face jiggled back and forth on his stomach. This guy ends up winning fan of the night and free tickets to the SEC Tournament. My sister helped win a fan free tickets to the SEC Tournament. We won that night and I called Bridget afterwards. She just laughed and was pleased to learn she was a focal point of the crowd.

Then, last year, my junior year, the Gator students repeated the "Bridget's Better" theme again. So, when you combine the fact that they have pictures of my sister and my reputation as a "Gator Killer," anything goes for this, my final trip to Gainesville and The Swamp.

The atmosphere in Florida is about as rough for an opposing player as it gets. Our bus pulls up to the "O'Dome," Florida's gym, and the fans are outside giving us gator chomps and throwing their middle fingers up. Many of them slept outside the arena to assure themselves a good seat for the game. You've got to appreciate the Florida fans. They are original, creative, and very passionate about their team. They do everything they can to create a harsh environment and a homecourt advantage.

I was the first to take the court for warmups, and the student section was packed and ready for the Volunteer arrival. The boos, the "Bradshaw, you suck," and the "Bridget's Better" chants began immediately. I laughed and decided to play along with them. So, I stepped to the free throw line for my first shot in warmups and intentionally shot an air ball wide left; not even close. The place erupted as if I had just given them everything they wanted in life.

This was a big night for the Florida fans. The air was electric because, in addition to the game, the fans were celebrating the fact that both their football and basketball teams were simultaneously national champions.

Florida jumped ahead with an early lead and played like defending National Champs. It was unbelievable how quickly they expanded the lead. Before we knew it, we were down 27 points…in the first half! We ended up fighting back in the second half, but never really got over the hump to cause them any fear. We lost by 16. But being close is no consolation prize worth having.

Coach Pearl articulated these thoughts in the locker room after the game when he said, "Yeah, sure you fought back in the second half and you never quit. But that's what is expected of you! Imagine if one of you did quit playing. Your ass wouldn't be on this team any more! So, I'm not going to pat you on the back for doing something you're supposed to do. We shouldn't have to get ourselves down early so we can wake up and decide to play."

February 5, Chris Lofton is Back

With everything that has happened this year it all comes down to an eight-game season. With eight conference games left, this is where teams will separate themselves and battle for the 65 NCAA tournament spots.

The big headline for this game is the return of Chris Lofton. He has missed the past four games with an ankle sprain. This was another injury to challenge our dedicated trainer, Chad Newman. It has been an eventful year for Chad, but there is no injury more important to the team than Chris Lofton's sprained ankle.

Chris and Chad have been doing everything possible to get his ankle healed as soon as possible. They meet in the morning before class, in between class, before practice, after practice, and then again at night. The dedication between the two has been amazing. Chad would laugh with Chris and tell him, "My job is on the line with your injury. You better hurry up and get on the court before I get fired for not having you healthy." I joked with Chad saying, "With as much time as Chris is taking out of your day, your wife must really be happy." Chad responded, "Yeah, Chris is my wife's least favorite player now. It used to be you, Dane. But now Chris is the reason why I can never get home at a reasonable hour." Of course he was joking but the injuries to Chris and me have led to many late evenings in the training room for treatment, causing Chad to work a lot of overtime. It takes the concerted effort of many people to make a Division I Basketball program successful. Chad is doing more than his part by getting Chris back in playing shape.

February 6, LSU Tigers

Our team couldn't wait to hear the roar of the crowd when Chris Lofton's name was announced. We felt just like our fans. Coach put him in the starting lineup. Chris is always the last name announced. It was set up as if it was a movie. The announcer introduced Chris and Thompson-Boling Arena erupted with the fans on their feet as they applauded like never before. Chris never really shows much emotion but you could tell how excited he was to be back on the court.

The first possession of the game Chris was fouled on a three and made all three free throws. After that, we never looked back. This was a great win for us and we made the most of an opportunity to separate ourselves from LSU when it comes down to Selection Sunday for the NCAA Tournament.

At this point, you are probably bored with me complaining about the way I play, but I am in an unbelievable shooting slump. I have made only five out of my last 35 shots. Perhaps this is a chance for a young fan or player to learn the importance of perseverance and doing what you can to help your team. All I know to do is to continue on the right path with hard work, dedication, and perseverance. I have to trust that it will all work out, but in the meantime I need to find a way to relax. Tonight, the most important thing is that we got ourselves a big win and we are one step closer to our goal—selection as NCAA Tournament participants. We want to demonstrate that we are one of the nation's best college basketball teams by successfully participating in March Madness.

February 7, Hard to Take a Day Off

We had the day off and a few friends suggested that I not even go to the gym today. They wanted me to take the day off and stay completely away from basketball. I thought it was a good idea; perhaps it would help clear my mind. It turned out that wasn't as easy as I thought. It did help me realize more than ever that everything I do revolves around basketball. And that's been true since I have been in elementary school.

I didn't go to the gym, but as soon as I turned on the television I couldn't help but watch basketball games. Then, when I switched on my computer, like an addicted person, I went to espn.com and looked at the men's basketball section to see how friends and former teammates were doing at their respective schools. After this, I watched SportsCenter for a recap of the day's basketball events. So, there was no getting away from the game of basketball for me.

However, my body seemed to appreciate the rest from the physical contact of the sport. Tomorrow we will start work, seeking revenge on the Vanderbilt Commodores.

February 10, Vanderbilt Commodores

One good thing about SEC East basketball is that you get a second chance to play your rivals. Whether this is an opportunity to sweep an opponent or retaliate for a loss, it is great not having to wait an entire year to play again as in football. To say we retaliated for Vanderbilt's earlier victory against us would be an understatement.

We started the game with some extremely hot shooting from the floor and they missed some open looks. That combination dug Vanderbilt a hole and they were never able to recover. We went on to win the game by 27 points!

The NCAA selection committee looks to see which teams have improved during the course of the season. Head-to-head match ups are key factors. There are still games to be played, but this win was so convincing and because it came later in the year, we definitely gained an edge over Vanderbilt.

This is why it is so important to continue to get better throughout the season and peak at the right time. What a team does during a season is important, but for a number of reasons it's more important to play well down the stretch. We laid the groundwork for success with some key wins earlier in the season, and our win today has hopefully given us the momentum and confidence to play well from now on. We believe things are looking up for our Tennessee Volunteer basketball team!

February 12, Bernard King

The big news of the day is that for the first time in 30 years, former Vol Bernard King will be returning to Knoxville to have his jersey retired. King was a three-time All-American from 1975-1977 and went on to lead the NBA in scoring, just to name a few of his many accomplishments. Many of us know that Bernard was a great player, but because we weren't even born during his days at Tennessee, we are unfamiliar with how he played the game. For that reason, Coach Pearl took time away from the Kentucky scout and put in a highlight tape from Bernard's playing days. As we watched, it was obvious, in terms of basketball skill, that he was a man amongst boys.

The Kentucky game was an excellent event to showcase Bernard's welcome back to Knoxville. In the history of Kentucky basketball, no team dominated them more than the teams led by Bernard King and Ernie Grunfield. We've often heard the story that after King lost to Kentucky his freshman year, he allegedly said, "As long as I'm at Tennessee we will never lose to Kentucky again." And guess what? They never did, as he went on to lead Tennessee to five straight wins over the Wildcats. Hopefully, we can honor him tomorrow night with a victory. It should be a magical atmosphere.

February 13, Kentucky Wildcats

Several times throughout the course of this season, our team has entered the court by coming through the stands of Thompson-Boling Arena. It's always a thrilling experience, but nothing would compare to tonight's walk through the crowd. Bernard King led the way and I was right behind him. I couldn't believe that I was following Bernard King's footsteps through a sold-out crowd to take the court against the Kentucky Wildcats. Sometimes you just have take a deep breath and soak it all in, and that is precisely what I did. And, the best parts were still ahead of us.

Bernard and many of his former teammates were in attendance for the retiring of King's jersey at halftime. We helped make their trip to Knoxville worthwhile. We went on to beat Kentucky by four on a night where Kentucky couldn't overcome the magical atmosphere. It was one of those nights where we felt destiny was on our side and our winning was preordained. It was the first time in my four years of playing that we beat Kentucky at home. Perhaps in the Coach Pearl era the UT program can regain dominance over Kentucky. In his first two seasons, Coach Pearl has a 2-2 record against the Wildcats.

Bernard King and Ernie Grunfield were both in the locker room after the game to help us celebrate. To our surprise, Ernie spoke to us, saying, "Congratulations guys, that was great." Then he joked, "but it's not better than beating them five out of six."

My struggles shooting the ball continued to haunt me, but I had nine assists and nothing was going to take away from the fact that our team had just beaten Kentucky and I was celebrating with "The Ernie and Bernie Show." With those legendary players in the same room, it was fun to be a fan. I had a photocopy of the *Sports Illustrated* cover graced by Bernard and Ernie. I didn't want to act like a little kid asking for an autograph, so using a couple of dollars I bribed Coach Forbes' son, Chris, to go ask for me. So, he goes up to Bernard and Ernie and says, "Dane Bradshaw wants you to sign this for him." My cover was blown (thanks Chris). We laughed about it, but the two legends gave me their autographs and I also had my picture taken with them.

The person behind all of this is Coach Pearl. He is the one responsible for bringing Bernard King back for the first time in 30 years. He is fully responsible for giving the former greats of Tennessee the appropriate respect they deserve. Most coaches wouldn't even think about what has happened in the distant past. Coach Pearl is different because he isn't just about the "Pearl Era." He stays grounded and is so appreciative of everyone else. The guy has completely turned the UT program around and just coached us to a huge win over Kentucky. But beyond winning games, Coach Pearl is also creating a true basketball family at Tennessee like it has never seen before. He gets a win over Kentucky at home while wearing an orange dress coat in honor of Coach Ray Mears and while bringing back Bernard King, Ernie Grunfeld and other players from that historic era. You never know what the coach is going to do next, but you know whatever it is, it will be aimed at helping UT basketball.

February 17, South Carolina Gamecocks

South Carolina has the worst conference record in the SEC, but as last year's NIT champion, we knew they would be a spoiler and cause a setback to some team's season. Unfortunately, that team was Tennessee. As much as our win versus Kentucky was a step forward, this loss may have been just as big of a step back. We extended our conference road record to 0-6, whereas last year we went 5-3 on the road. It isn't our style of play that is causing us to struggle on the road because last year's road record proved that we can be successful away from home. Youth and immaturity may be a factor, but I think it is our overall lack of commitment as players. At home, the crowd is behind us, constantly encouraging us to have the necessary intensity to win games. On the road we miss our fan encouragement and struggle to play with the consistency we need.

To show you how quickly things can change, if you recall after the Vanderbilt win I reported that we may have gained an edge over Vanderbilt as the team that got better over the season. Today Vanderbilt beats top-ranked Florida for the biggest win of the college basketball weekend while we take a loss to lowly South Carolina. So, on one Saturday of basketball the situation has reversed. Now, Vanderbilt has almost guaranteed itself a spot in the NCAA tournament, while we are still perched on the selection committee bubble. This is SEC basketball. One day you're up and the next day you're fighting for your postseason life. This is our situation as we prepare to face and overcome adversity with a home game against Alabama—a team Tennessee has not beaten in its last seven meetings.

February 19, Preparing for Alabama

Coach Pearl has such a dominating, intimidating demeanor that I believe many outsiders assume that practices after a loss are worse than they are. He tells it like it is and makes no attempt to disguise his displeasure with substandard effort, but he knows we are young players and realizes the importance of maintaining our confidence throughout the season. With no doubts, we know he deeply cares for us and he looks for ways to put positive thoughts in our heads.

For example, as Coach shifted the focus to Alabama he pointed out that we have an opportunity to make history. We could tie the record for most wins in a season at Thompson-Boling Arena, 15, and we have an opportunity to beat Alabama, which is something the last six Tennessee teams haven't been able to do. Beyond these opportunities is the chance, with another win against a ranked opponent, to strengthen our resume for the NCAA tournament.

February 21, Alabama Crimson Tide

Repeatedly, we keep telling ourselves, "This is the biggest game of the year." Down the stretch, however, when you are a "bubble team," scrambling for selection to the NCAA tournament, every game *is* the most important of the year. I'm sure Alabama echoed this same motivational thought in their locker room. But tonight, the Tennessee Vols were victorious.

We didn't roll over the Tide as it took overtime to finish them off. The game was sloppy as Alabama committed 26 turnovers and we shot only 33 percent from the floor. The arena was pulsating with the emotion of our fans, who were a tremendous factor in helping us eke out this victory.

My scoring/shooting slump continued. I apologize for discussing it again, but I promised to try to portray a true insider's view of the game. And my current view is being warped by frustration over my poor shooting, which in turn is detrimental to our team. I know I bring some positive values to the team with my experience, effort, ball-handling, and defensive intensity, but it would be much better if I could make some shots. The result is that I don't feel like I'm contributing with the rest of my teammates. Even with all the support I have around me, I can't help but be embarrassed and ashamed of my play.

However, whenever I get down like this, my mind tells me that I've worked hard and am doing my best. Further, in the big scheme of life, if a shooting slump is the toughest thing I have to deal with, then I must be a fortunate guy. One thing for certain, I'm sure as hell not giving up.

February 24, Arkansas Razorbacks

"Win it to get in it." This was the theme and goal we took into this game because victory would give us 20 wins, eight wins in the SEC, and a much needed SEC road win. Consequently, we felt if we won this game we would get into the NCAA tournament.

After a hard-fought first half, Arkansas led us 36-33. They opened the second half with a dunk, adding to their lead. But, we dug in on defense and used our full-court press and traps, forcing them into 24 turnovers, 17 in the second half. Chris lit it up with 31 points. Both JaJuan and Wayne had solid nights, scoring 16 and 14 points, respectively.

We built our lead to 12 points, but the Razorbacks are an excellent team and wouldn't lay down. They stormed back to within three points. The score was 73-70 in our favor with a couple of minutes left to play. We had a number of guys make huge hustle plays. JaJuan and Ramar collaborated on one play in particular that seemed to take some of the life out of the Razorbacks. JaJuan deflected a pass and Ramar, hustling in from behind, tipped it ahead to JaJuan for an easy layup on the other end. If you expect to win, these are the kind of plays that you have to make on the road in SEC competition. Through poise and consistent play, we were able to accomplish our goal of "Win it to get in it."

We celebrated the win in the locker room. I felt there was a collective sigh of relief more than anything else. We did not want to be stuck at 19 wins, heading into a matchup with Florida and then a final road game at Georgia. I don't want to use the word relax, but the rest of the regular season will be much less stressful, knowing that we seem to have done enough to get into the Big Dance.

It had not been since the Louisiana-Lafayette game that we were able to enjoy a flight back to Knoxville, so I played a small joke on Coach Shay and Coach Forbes. They are two awesome guys, but aren't in the same physical shape as they were in their collegiate playing days. Forbes tells people he is on a "seafood diet." What's the seafood diet, you ask? He responds, "See food, eat it!" Anyway, as we approached Knoxville, I asked the flight attendant to announce a message over the intercom that read, "Due to lack of equipment, in case of emergency we will be using passengers Steve Forbes and Jason Shay as flotation devices." She went along with the joke and we all landed with a laugh. I'm sure my retribution from Coach Shay and Forbes will arrive when I least expect it.

February 26, Looking Forward to Senior Night

Senior Night and the Florida game are right around the corner. This game will be an opportunity for me to enjoy the **Volunteer Fans** one last time at Thompson-Boling Arena. Today, I did an interview that will be played on the Jumbotron tomorrow night. The interview was a chance to show my appreciation for all of the fans, but there was not enough time for me to say what I wanted to tell the fans, so I'll use this book to try and put into words how special the fans have been for me.

One may wonder how I could have much good to say about my first two seasons. We barely made the NIT during my freshman year and finished 14-17 my second season. Our coaching staff and players on those two teams tried hard, but we couldn't seem to bring the intensity and consistency needed to win. Thus, we suffered through two mediocre seasons. I think because both the fans and I went through those losing seasons together, it has made these past two seasons that much more memorable to share. I am proud to say that I am one of the few players that has experienced the tough times before enjoying the victorious seasons Coach Pearl and his staff have provided. Knoxville and the University community have embraced me in a way that I could never have imagined.

Every ounce of support that people have shown for our program and for me personally has been greatly appreciated. That includes fans waiting for autographs, those who would simply say, "Good game," and the big-time donors who have provided our team with the best facilities there are to offer. **Thank you all!**

Whenever we struggled this season, all we had to do was come to Thompson-Boling where our fans brought us back to life. The fans have led us to an undefeated season thus far at home, 15-0. Without this, we don't achieve our goal of competing in the NCAA tournament. A win tomorrow night would break the record for most games won in a season at Thompson-Boling. While it's a tall order, I hope we can share another victory with our fans in my final home game.

One of the stories surrounding Senior Night is that Coach Pearl will be announcing a scholarship named in my honor, representing the model of a true student-athlete. He will fund the $100,000 scholarship himself. I could say I can't believe it, but I'm not surprised by his generosity. I am amazed, but not surprised. I have to believe there have been other "Dane Bradshaws" in college basketball before, but only one Dane Bradshaw was blessed enough to have a coach like Bruce Pearl who would be this generous.

In two short seasons, Bruce Pearl has revamped our mediocre and little publicized basketball program, to a nationally ranked and recognized program. Few know how many hours of hard and meaningful work he has contributed toward this success. He is known for his outgoing personality, but it has never been about Bruce Pearl. He gets the most joy out of making others feel good and bringing happiness to others' lives. The scholarship he has named in honor of me is a perfect example of his unique mindset and generosity. If there were more people like **Mr. Bruce Pearl**, the world would be a better place. The entire Pearl family has been phenomenal and have done favors for me that my family and I will never be able to return.

My family will be in attendance to share the night with me. It's not like my family is just now showing up for Senior Night; they have been there for me my entire life.

Basketball made our already strong, tight-knit family even closer. My family bonded and showed support for one another through basketball. All my siblings played collegiate basketball at one level or another and are the coolest, nicest people you could ever be around. They are responsible for any toughness I exert on the court as I was the beneficiary of being the youngest of four who wasn't cut any slack. We were very competitive playing basketball in our driveway games, but we were always each other's biggest fans and wanted the best for one another. Basketball has provided some of the greatest memories in my life, but my fondest memories are those times spent with my two brothers and sister. My first memories were them playing basketball, so I just went with the flow. All I have ever wanted to do is be like them.

The *greatest contribution to my development as a player* were the two-on-two games between my siblings in the driveway of our home. These games were extremely competitive and would usually end with one of us storming into the house in frustration. Bridget was the toughest match-up during my young career. And Cody and Ryan never took it easy on me; no matter what I did I could never beat them.

All of my siblings are truly my heros and best friends. The advice, criticism, support and tough love they have given me is the main reason for any success I have achieved. I don't even want to know where I'd be without them.

Brothers, Ryan and Cody, and sister, Bridget, have all traveled to Knoxville to share and show their support for my big night. Ryan drove from Memphis, Cody flew in from San Francisco, and Bridget flew in from D.C.

My parents, Mike and Linda, deserve more applause than anyone tomorrow night. To say that they are supportive would be an understatement. They are the captains of our family and responsible for any compliments paid to us. I can't begin to describe what they have meant to their children. There is a fine line that parents must watch when it comes to supporting a child or pushing her or him too far. My parents were unbelievably supportive and never crossed that line. I believe this is a main reason why I never burned out on the sport of basketball. My parents never cared about statistics or measurement of results, they simply asked that we give 100 percent.

They make the six-hour drive from Memphis to Knoxville every game and travel to every road game as well. Distance or game site has never been an issue; from Maui to Starkville, Mississippi, they have been there. I thanked fans before but there are no bigger, more loyal fans than my parents. I am so blessed and appreciative to have them in my life.

It seems that many people respect my unselfishness, hustle, and work ethic more than anything. This is how my parents taught me to live. Fortunately, I have been able to demonstrate these traits through basketball. All my life, mom and dad have stressed using the talents the Lord has given us as best as we could and to give 100 percent effort in everything we do.

Dad is one of the most unselfish people you could ever meet. He has always been charitable to others in need, even when he was struggling financially early in his business career. Mom is the same way. For example, if there was a new kid at school who was having a hard time fitting in, it was Mom who would step in and invite him over to our house, asking me to reach out in a friendly way. Basketball has been a wonderful stage for me to show what my family and upbringing are all about.

Someone who is as much a part of my extended family as anyone is my high school coach, Terry Tippett. He has also made the drive to Knoxville with his wife, Nancy. Coach Tippett is responsible for molding me as a player and the qualities of my game have stemmed from his teachings. His system at White Station was always centered around the team-first mentality and his knowledge of the game helped develop my basketball I.Q. The person I could best compare Coach Tippett to is Indianapolis Colts coach, Tony Dungy. He never cursed, he did things the right way, he is a man of great faith, and he was successful in this approach. Coach Tippett has been one of the most influential people in my life and is a prime example of how fortunate I have been to be surrounded by such great and caring people.

February 27, Florida Gators & Senior Night

A Pulitzer Prize-winning author couldn't have scripted the night better. It was a most unique, surreal Senior Night; one I could never have imagined.

Dick Vitale was in the house for the first time in my career to provide game commentary to an ESPN national audience. If Dicky V was here, this meant, tonight, our game was the biggest game in college basketball.

I took the court early to get some extra shots up and I walked out to the roar of the student section. Since I am the only senior on our team, the focus of Senior Night, necessarily, is on me. A few students had painted their chest in my honor, while others held up mini posters that simply read, "Thanks Dane." It was more attention than I expected, especially since it was still an hour-and-a-half before the game. But, this was just the beginning of a thrilling night.

Peyton Manning was in town for the game and he brought fellow Super Bowl champions Jeff Saturday and Brandon Stokely with him. Peyton gave us a pregame talk in the locker room; we sat and hung on every word he said. A lot of people can talk about the importance of teamwork and unselfishness, but when the Super Bowl MVP speaks everyone pays closer attention and takes it to heart. Peyton told us that this past season he didn't work any harder or watch any more film than he had in the past, but the biggest difference was the trust inside the locker room. In the past, he felt like as long as he played well or had the ball in his hands then the team had a chance. He learned that it would take more than that to win a championship. He told us the growing trust among teammates to do each other's part or to pickup the slack in given situations was the key difference that led to their championship season. His main message was to be unselfish and trust one another. We all were appreciative of his time and words and were able to apply it to the actual game.

Next, it was time for the pregame Senior Night ceremony. Coach Pearl had a prerecorded message on the Jumbotron in which he emphasized that this wasn't goodbye because we still have work to do. He went on to thank me and give me some of the greatest compliments I could have received, speaking as only Bruce Pearl can. My own interview combined with highlights from my career followed Coach Pearl's words. Finally, they announced my name and my family, and we walked out to center court with the noise of 24,000 cheering fans ringing in our ears. I felt like the most blessed person in the world and we hadn't even started the game.

ESPN commentators Dick Vitale and Brad Nessler came to mid-court and shook my hand in congratulations. This was a touching, professional gesture. Coach Pearl and I hugged as they announced the scholarship. I wasn't as emotional for this as I thought I would be. Neither was Coach Pearl. We later discussed the scene and agreed that we were on the same page. We were both appreciative, but very anxious to take the court versus Florida. I was unbelievably thankful for what was happening, but it just wasn't time for me to reflect on everything. It was time to do our best to beat Florida.

As the game began, we got off to a great start and never looked back.

The story of the night may have been Coach Pat Summitt. At the first media timeout she returned a favor to Coach Pearl for painting his chest at the Lady Vol-Duke game. Coach Summitt came to the court dressed in a cheerleader's outfit and she wore a hat with a feather boa wrapped around it. She led the crowd as they sang "Rocky Top" together. Then it was time for her grand finale—she was hoisted to the top of a cheerleader pyramid and held her hands up to the crowd as if she hadn't missed a beat since her junior high cheerleading days. It was great to see another side of Coach Summitt.

During these festivities, our team had trouble paying attention to Coach Pearl's play calling. It was a happy, hysterical time as the crowd got to enjoy the lighter side of Coach Summitt, including her planting a feathered hat on Dicky-V's bald head. But, somehow we managed to stay focused on our business at hand, returning the whopping that Florida had given us earlier in the season.

Our team couldn't believe how well the night was going as we extended the lead to 27 points. However, the Gators made a run, as they always seem to do, and cut the lead to eight. But we managed to hang on. My proudest moment of the game was a steal to somewhat "ice" the game. Corey Brewer drove to the baseline and I immediatcly recognized the play from watching film. I ran across the court to intercept a pass that I knew was coming. Brewer pivoted and threw the pass just like he was supposed to do. I wasn't even in the right defensive position but I was so sure of the play that I instinctively ran over to make the steal. I was fouled and made both free throws.

As much as I have suffered with the inadequacy of my own play, to walk off the court with a win against Florida on Senior Night and be as satisfied with my play was absolutely storybook.

Maybe it was coincidence, but I believe that the continued hard work, faith and perseverance was rewarded at the perfect time. I believe that it goes back to what Allan Houston said to our team earlier in the season, "The Lord blesses obedience."

Blue Ribbon Basketball Yearbook editor Chris Dortch said to me after the game, "That was years of karma built up right there. Congratulations." Dortch has been one of the nicest, kindest people I have come across in my career. He was the one who recommended me to the All-Glue team selected by Seth Davis of *Sports Illustrated*. I met Davis in person after the game. We had spoken over the phone, but it's satisfying to meet a high profile figure in the sports world who is as humble and courteous as Seth Davis. The All-Glue team honors those players who keep their team intact, yet often go unnoticed. Being selected as captain of the All-Glue team by Seth Davis was an unexpected and greatly appreciated honor.

If the night was not already a fairytale, my family and I had the opportunity to celebrate with Peyton Manning and the Colts players. As expected, they were as cool as could be and helped make my night so special.

In the years to come, there may be a senior who makes a buzzer shot to win the game as he scores 50 points on Senior Night. That would still be small in comparison to the environment that surrounded my experience. Dick Vitale commentating; a pregame speech and postgame celebration with Super Bowl MVP Peyton Manning; a ceremony all to myself as the lone senior; a $100,000 scholarship named in my honor, compliments of Bruce and Kim Pearl; Pat Summitt as a cheerleader; a satisfying individual performance and all of this capped by an electrifying win over Florida in front of 24,000 sensational fans and a national TV audience. *Wow!!* Realizing I've spent so much time with self-doubt, self-pity and self-disappointment, this was an unbelievably wonderful experience. Perhaps all of us spend too much energy dwelling on our shortcomings. Anyway, this was in my heart:

Thank you, Knoxville!

Thank you, University of Tennessee!

Thank you, Pearls!

Most of all, thank you Bradshaw family for being there for this night! To me the most comforting thought about the night was knowing that my family would have been here, no matter the circumstances.

March 3, Georgia Bulldogs

The grand finale to our season's play, was an away game with the Georgia Bulldogs. In some ways, it didn't have the aura of a grand finale. I suppose that's partly due to the fact that our sensational victory against Florida virtually assured us of selection to play in the NCAA tournament. So in a way this game didn't have the urgency of our previous seven games. But there was still a lot at stake above and beyond our pride and will to win. A win would tie us with Vanderbilt for second place in the SEC East, and would give us a higher seed in the upcoming SEC tournament. It would also further demonstrate that we could win on the road, which had been one of our season's shortcomings.

I actually forgot this was going to be my last game on an opponent's home court. But before the game, I realized this was somewhat of a senior night for me on the road, as well. The welcoming was quite different than it was last Tuesday night at Thompson-Boling Arena. Here, I took the court for warmups to a chorus of boos and derogatory remarks. This kind of reaction from the opposing teams' fans has been a staple of my career. By responding to the crowd and hecklers, part of this is my fault. For some strange reason, I have enjoyed the heckling and will miss being booed and being insulted. Most of the heckling has been in fun as opposed to being mean-spirited. At least it has been fun for me, and I don't believe either the fans or I have crossed the line of controversy or unsportsmanlike behavior. Here at Georgia it made me think, "What will I miss more, the cheers or the boos?"

During the course of the game, Georgia threw quite a few runs at us but we answered all of them. It was a close game until Georgia was eventually forced to begin fouling out of desperation. We always try to get the ball in the hands of our best free throw shooters in situations like these (Chris, JaJuan, or Jordan.) However, sometimes the opponents won't foul these guys. I had to smile inwardly when the ball got passed back to me and the Georgia coach yelled, "Foul him! Foul him!" This is insulting but I have earned it with my poor free throw percentage. Fortunately, I hit both free throws and for one last time I was able to experience the beautiful silence of an opposing team's home crowd in silence. Road wins are very sweet. We were able to get our win and get back to Knoxville.

Section III — Postseason Play

March 7, SEC Tournament

The team is sprawled out across the bus as we head to Atlanta for the SEC Tournament. It is well known that "SEC Tournament" and "Tennessee success" are never mentioned in the same breath. Since 1992, when the tournament format was changed, Tennessee has the worst SEC Tournament winning percentage in the league.

During my career, we have a record of 1-3 in the SEC tournament. The current team, players and staff shouldn't be held responsible for what has haunted Tennessee in the past, but hopefully we can do something to change our losing image. That opportunity will come tomorrow night at 9:45 when we do battle with LSU.

We defeated LSU earlier in the season at home, but this is a very tough draw. LSU has underachieved this season by finishing last in the SEC West, but they were a Final Four team a year ago. Glen "Big Baby" Davis, who has been injured the past couple of weeks, is a former SEC Player of the Year and will be back healthy just in time for us. Only time will tell, but I hope that I haven't overpacked for the SEC Tournament for the fourth year in a row.

March 8, LSU Tigers

It was another short-lived trip at the SEC Tournament. Disappointment doesn't seem to be a powerful enough word for how we feel right now. It was a hard-fought game that we lost in overtime, as Glen Davis put the LSU team on his back and helped bull their way to a 76-67 win. Chris Lofton carried us, but we simply didn't provide him enough help. We can't depend on him to win games by himself, especially in postseason play. Some other guys made key plays to help force overtime, but overall we didn't bring the team effort needed to win.

There are a number of reasons why this loss stings more than others. We hate it for the fans who traveled down to Atlanta or planned to make the trip for the weekend. I'm sure every year they are thinking, "This will be the year." I can't explain UT's consistent lack of success in the SEC Tournament, but I feel confident that Coach Pearl, in the near future, will change UT's losing pattern in this tournament. I just hate that I can't be a part of this change when that day comes.

One thing a player can take pride in through his career is helping to improve a program's situation. In this case, I was unable to be a part of any positive changes to Tennessee's performances at the SEC Tournament.

Tournament losses are the worst, because unlike conference play there are no rematches; therefore, chances for redemption are not possible. For various reasons, after finishing in the Final Four last season and being ranked in the preseason top ten, LSU's current season has been less than successful. So, understandably, they took great pleasure in knocking us down a notch.

We missed an opportunity at the SEC Tournament, but our team will do what we always do. We will go back home and get to work. The reality is that all of our hard work, sacrifices, wins and losses to date were primarily directed toward winning two NCAA tournament games next weekend. By advancing to the Sweet 16, a basketball program marks its place in the history books. And, hopefully, this achievement would lay the groundwork for even greater UT success.

March 10, NCAA Tournament Play

For the first time in months we had a practice where all we did was focus on what we do. With NCAA Selection Sunday coming up tomorrow, we have no scouting report to go over and the only thing we can do to prepare is to focus on us. We are all extremely anxious to learn how the Selection Committee seeds our team and who our early opponents will be.

Last year, I remember there was a high possibility that we were going to be matched up with the coaching staff's former school, University of Wisconsin-Milwaukee. Our coaches were all praying that we were not going to face their former players and friends. This year, Coach Forbes has a similar fear. Many bracketologists have predicted that we could possibly meet Texas A&M in the second round. It is hard enough for a coach to leave a program, but to have to play them in a "win or go home" situation would be a form of mental torture.

I believe we will be seeded no lower than number five. Without being too biased, I think we are the second most attractive team in the SEC behind Florida. If the SEC is rated the number one RPI conference in the country and we have the second best resume in the conference, I don't see how we could be seeded any lower than a number five seed. There is not much difference between a number four or a number five seed. Both should have favorable first-round matchups and, if they win, would have to face one another in the second round. We could have helped our seeding level at the SEC tournament, but because Vanderbilt and Kentucky were also eliminated early, our first-round loss in the SEC tournament should have little impact on our NCAA seed. The Selection Show begins at 6 p.m. tomorrow, and it can't come soon enough.

Without the contributions of our freshmen, there is no way our team would be waiting for Selection Sunday with such high expectations. Associate Head Coach Tony Jones has to be credited for much of our team's success. His ability to recruit freshmen that were ready to make an impact right away has been vital to our winning season. For our team to maintain the high level of play required to be selected for NCAA tournament play, after losing the players we lost from last year's team, is a tremendous compliment to Coach Jones. His future is extremely bright and I am sure he will be a top prospect for head coaching openings at season's end.

March 11, Selection Sunday

Without question, this is one of the coolest, most exhilarating days of the year. The anxiety is at an all-time high as we sit and wait for our school's name to pop up on the screen. You don't know who you're playing, where you're playing, or when you're playing. At least we aren't a bubble team, so we will not have to wonder and worry *IF* we are going to be playing at all.

Selection Sunday is thrilling because the basketball stakes are high and the suspense builds as you wait for the name of your school to be called. The event produces a unique type of intensity. It all hits you at once as the announcers say, "The University of Tennessee."

We gathered as a team along with several members of the athletic department and donors at the East Side Club Level in Neyland Stadium. The Selection Show began and it seemed like every time I thought they were going to call our name, they didn't. Eventually, there was only the South region left so we now knew by the process of elimination that we would be playing in the South region. Finally, the CBS announcer said, "The number five seed, The University of Tennessee." Of course, there was a huge ovation in the room. All I could do was continue to focus on the screen to see who our opponent was. Then, there it was—Long Beach State.

Every team in the NCAA tournament is there because they are a good team. But, at first glance, there were more intimidating teams that we could be facing than Long Beach State. Without being overconfident, I was pleased with our draw. The game site is in Columbus, Ohio, so we will be as close to home as we could have hoped, which is another pleasing fact.

We were all excited, but it seemed there was a much more businesslike approach among the team than anything. We know we missed an opportunity last year to get to the Sweet 16 and we were ready to do anything we could to not allow that to happen again.

It wasn't long until the coaches went back to the office to immediately start scouting our opponent. I wondered how they could get game film on an opponent like Long Beach State so quickly. I found that our staff has every single televised college basketball game recorded throughout the season. That isn't just the games that you see on basic cable, but every game that is on college basketball game-plan packages. Throughout the year Long Beach State had played seven games that were televised. This gave Coach Pearl and the staff plenty of film to decipher tonight, and we will begin preparing as a team tomorrow at practice.

It was such an unbelievable day to be a part of college basketball. I couldn't imagine being a senior in a basketball program and being left out of an amazing day like this. It wasn't too long ago that I was sitting around, knowing that we had no chance of a postseason bid. I believe that experience makes me and some of my teammates that much more grateful for our present opportunity. This started me thinking about when I was a kid and what teams I dreamed of playing for in the NCAA tournament. I was a big fan of Michigan State and Syracuse and dreamed of playing for those teams. Yet here I am at The University of Tennessee with a much higher seed than Michigan State, and Syracuse didn't even make the tournament. Poof! The time for nostalgic remembrances is over; it's time for all of us to focus on beating Long Beach State.

March 14, Off to the Big Dance

Usually we charter a flight, but with so many people traveling we took a larger plane. This caused us to have to go through airport security and other delays that we are able to skip when using charter flights. However, no one complained as we received our seat assignments. All the players were assigned first class seating, which is something none of us had ever experienced. The guys were excited and we had no problem letting the other UT passengers know that we were higher on the seating ladder than they were. We made a host of comments such as, "I'll send you some peanuts back there in the *coach section*," or asking the flight attendant, "Could you close the curtain so we can be more secluded from those lower class passengers." It was only a 50-minute flight, but we took advantage of every minute we had in first class.

The extra perks didn't stop there. In the NCAA Tournament, the team bus has a police escort as we go to and from practices and games. With the motorcycle police leading the way, we flew through every red light and caused other cars on the highway to pull to the side of the road. What should have been a 30-minute drive was about 15 minutes with a police escort. The players were loving how our bus dominated the roadways as if the President was in town.

The team arrived at the arena early for practice, because we had media obligations. The usual questions were asked but Chris had a humorous answer when he and I were being interviewed by the CBS commentators. They asked, "Can you compare the difference between a couple of years ago with a half empty Thompson-Boling Arena to a sold out Thompson-Boling Arena nowadays?" Chris began by giving a politically correct answer by saying, "Well, it's great to see it turn around and it's fun to play in front of a sellout crowd," but then the truth came out as he revealed a reality, "You know, a couple years ago it was so dead you could hear peoples' conversations in the stands while you were playing. The fans had to be careful what they said about us because we could hear them." We all laughed at that response.

Later in the evening, we had a film session and afterward Coach Pearl had a few words. I think he felt the need to make us have greater respect for Long Beach State. He said that guys playing for them have a chip on their shoulder. They were good enough to play at UCLA or California but were overlooked and didn't get the same opportunity as us. This is their opportunity. He compared the team to himself, "Hell, I'm a Division II guy. Does that mean I wasn't as good as these other coaches at top programs? Same thing goes for these players and coaches at Long Beach State." The message was clear. I don't think any of us were overlooking Long Beach State, but there was a need to put a little more fear in us without undermining our confidence.

Many people asked me if I felt nervous. I really couldn't answer because I felt more anxious than nervous. Finally I found my answer when Coach Pearl said, "The Sweet 16 is so close you can taste it." I realized that is exactly how I was feeling. I felt so confident in our team that I could "taste" the Sweet 16.

March 16, Round 1 of NCAA Tournament, Long Beach State 49ers

Before the game, there was no need for great motivational speeches. We all knew what was at stake. People predicted that this would be a high-scoring affair, but I'm not sure anyone expected what happened. Both teams began the game by scorching one another from the three-point line. Chris started off on fire but got a tough break as he was called for a charge, giving him his second foul in the first half. With Chris on the bench in foul trouble, we managed to hang on to a 12 point lead at halftime. Long Beach State ran out of answers for our weapons as we put on an offensive show scoring 121 points to their 86. Chris, JaJuan, and Ramar each had 20-plus points and I had a career high 11 assists, but we all knew that it was all about the win rather than personal stats.

With a number of offensive highlights, there was none greater than Tanner Wild's deep three pointer as time expired. As a walk-on, this had to be a great reward for Tanner as the crowd and bench erupted when he banged a three-point basket in the NCAA tournament. It wasn't just a three-point basket, rather it was *the three point basket* that allowed our team to score 121 points and tie the school record for scoring the most points of any team in the history of UT.

We all shared in the moment, but I expect it meant the most to our walk-on players. Ben, Rick, Justin, Quinn, and Tanner have paid the price as much as any one of the starting players. They go through everything we do, knowing that chances of playing time are slim. They are willing to do whatever is needed for the team without the recognition or spotlight. It's always great when they get an opportunity to play in the game. Contrary to the belief of some, these guys can really play. There have been plenty of times in my four years as a varsity player where the scout team, mostly walk-ons, have whopped up on the starters, forcing us to run sprints. Many of the walk-ons are good enough to be starters at smaller universities but chose this route. All the starters and coaches have a tremendous amount of respect for the walk-ons and were thrilled that Tanner knocked down a three in the NCAA tournament.

Our preseason goal of making the Sweet 16 was now so close we could really taste it. We needed only one more victory.

March 18, Round Two of NCAA Tournament
Virginia Cavaliers

Tip off is scheduled for 12:50 p.m. so we had an early wake up call and breakfast. I have never seen so much energy at 8 a.m. from our players. We definitely showed signs of a team that was ready to advance in the tournament.

CBS had a special feature on Chris before the game. I remember when Pink told me that CBS was in town and wanted to interview me. I thought, "Sweet. I'm getting a CBS interview." I was excited as I met with the CBS representative and cameramen and before I could sit down he said, "All right, we're doing a special on Chris." I should have known that was coming, I don't know what I was thinking. Most of the time whenever I sit down with a writer or analyst to talk about the team or me, they start off, "Dane, tell me a little about Chris." Chris deserves everything he gets and I have no problem telling anybody how great a player and great a guy he is, but it is funny how a majority of my interviews are about him.

Game time was nearing, but it couldn't come quick enough for us. This was the same exact day last year that we lost to Wichita State. Since that loss, it has been amazing that for an entire year we have busted our butts with 6 a.m. workouts, stadium runs with weight vests, and 9 p.m. night shooting. All of this effort aimed for this one game. Then I thought, "This isn't about what you have been working all year for. This is about what you have been working for your whole life." I felt like my whole legacy as a basketball player rested on this one game.

The game was a nail biter. It went back-and-forth as the teams exchanged the lead. Huge, clutch plays were made for both sides. Coach always says that we are best when everyone contributes and that was the deciding factor as we all played our roles relatively well. Ryan hit two clutch free throws causing

Virginia to play from behind in the final minute, fouling at every opportunity. Many times we think about how tough it would be to stand on the free throw line and knock down *two* free throws on a stage like the NCAA tournament to send your team to the Sweet 16. Try making *SIX.* That's exactly what Chris Lofton did. How many times in a row can you ask a guy to come through under pressure? Chris has ice water in his veins. He fought to get open, knowing they were going to foul him as soon as he touched the ball. Inbounding the ball can be a thankless job, but when you have a guy like Chris who wants the ball in these situations it makes my job much easier.

Down by three, Virginia guard Sean Singletary raced up the court and just barely misfired on a game tying three-point attempt. I was under the basket as the shot was in the air and, from my view, it looked like we were heading to overtime. But, as the buzzer sounded, we escaped with a three-point victory.

There was the high-fiving, hugging, dancing, chanting, anything you could imagine in the locker room as we celebrated. Pink hugged me and jokingly said, "You just sold a lot of books today!"

It was a special moment in University of Tennessee men's basketball history and I felt blessed to be sharing in the moment. We all celebrated, but quickly realized that we wanted more for the team. Many of our players have won state and other championships, and now that we had made it this far, we wanted more. Having said that, this was a remarkable day for Tennessee basketball and the UT faithful.

March 20, New Goals

Coach spoke to us at practice and reminded us that before the season started we had goals of winning the SEC and going to the Sweet 16. Now, he told us, "It was time to set new goals. We have another four-team tournament ahead of us in San Antonio to advance to the Final Four." The four teams were Ohio State, Memphis, Texas A&M and UT. We knew we were capable of beating either of these teams. Why? We had already beaten Memphis despite their gaudy 32-3 won-lost record and fifth-place national ranking. We hadn't played Texas A&M, but three of their season losses were to teams we had beaten—LSU, Texas and Memphis. Coach Forbes came to us from Texas A&M, which should be a plus factor for us if we meet up with them. We played Ohio State (first place, national ranking) to a standstill on their own floor. So we knew we not only earned our way to the Sweet 16; *we belonged there.* We were capable of beating any of these teams. Why not us?

March 22, Sweet 16, Ohio State Buckeyes

Our game doesn't tip off until 9 p.m. central time. We are able to sleep in with a brunch set up for us at 10:30 a.m., but there is a continental breakfast earlier in the morning for those of us who can't sleep that late. We all met for brunch and then had a quick film session from 11-11:30 a.m.

After the film session we have an hour of study hall, not exactly the most popular hour of the day. But Coach does his best to prevent us from getting behind in our classes while on the road. Following study hall, we have a 45 minute break before going to the Alamodome for our shootaround. We are allowed to have the court for an hour and then come back to the hotel for more film and our pregame meal. After all of this, we focus on just getting our legs up and getting plenty of rest before tipoff.

The late game time isn't very popular among the players because we would much rather get to business, but this is a typical day on the road before a late game.

Finally, it was time to get the show on the road. The atmosphere was sensational and it definitely had the feel of a big-time sports event. I and my teammates were living a dream. We jumped out on the Buckeyes early and played as good a half of basketball as we have all year. Everyone was contributing and that is when we are at our best. We shocked Ohio State and most of the sports world as we had a 17 point lead at the half. We confidently jogged back to the locker room.

At halftime in our locker room, it is commonplace to hear the simple phrase, "Down 10." This reminds us to not get comfortable with our lead and to play as if we were down by 10 points. However, this is not how we started the second half. The starters did a terrible job of setting the tempo early and establishing our team as the aggressor.

Ohio State quickly cut the lead to 10, and, before we knew it, we were in for a fight to the finish. Our defense was nonexistent in the second half, which is extremely frustrating. Sometimes your shot won't fall or you mishandle the ball, but defense is something you can control. Like Coach Pearl says, "Control what you can control." Because of our lack of urgency on the defensive end, we put ourselves in a tough position. With three minutes to go, we are tied with the number one team in the nation, so we still felt good about our chances. We again tied it with 38 seconds left on the clock. With a 35-second shot clock, Ohio State could wind the clock down in hopes for a last-second shot with little time to spare. Their point guard, Mike Conley, drove to the basket and was fouled with six seconds left. He made the first and we called a timeout to set up a play in the huddle.

We planned to get the ball in Ramar's hands and have him push it up the court with Wayne setting him a flat screen near half court. This would pull seven-foot shot-blocker Greg Oden away from the basket and give Ramar a more opportune path to the basket. At the same time, we would have Lofton set up in the opposite corner. If the man guarding Chris moved over to help stop Ramar's penetration, then Chris could be open for a three. Mike Conley stepped to the line and missed his second free throw off the back iron. In hindsight, we would rather Conley had made the free throw, because his miss disrupted our timing of the playcall. We still could have executed, but the missed shot caused us all to be in somewhat of a cluster. After he snagged the rebound, Ramar drove the full length of the court, similar to our earlier game against Ohio State. Unfortunately, when Ramar got to the basket, Oden was there to block the shot. The buzzer sounded, and the referee signaled the game was over.

At that moment, the life was taken out of me and the rest of our team. In the sport of basketball, nothing can take your legs out from under you like losing on a buzzer shot. Here we had blown a huge lead, and Ohio State had beaten us in the final seconds, just like they had done on their home court.

For me, in an instant, all hope was gone and my basketball career was over. I thought I could handle defeat, but I couldn't. Not like this. I untucked my jersey and pulled it over my face. I couldn't believe what had just happened; it didn't seem fair; it didn't seem real. The Elite Eight was in our hands and we let it go. I would have rather been down 10 points the whole game to a team like North Carolina and lose. The way we lost is perhaps the most painful, heartbreaking way possible.

At the beginning of the season, I and my teammates felt like the Sweet 16 would have been enough. I guess for a true competitor, nothing is enough unless you win it all. That's how our locker room felt. I wish I could remember what Coach Pearl said after the game, but I was in a whole other world with the towel around my face trying to hold myself together. There were more than a few tears as we huddled up one last time, "Together on three; One, Two, Three, TOGETHER!" Everyone felt the pain of the loss as we tried to support one another. Players, managers, trainers, and coaches put their arms around me while bracing me with kind words, but I couldn't give the thanks like I wanted to. My emotions wouldn't allow me to get a word out.

I was physically and emotionally drained as we got to the hotel where my parents, as always, met me with open arms. At 22 years old, my parents embraced me the same way they did when I was a 11-year old boy getting eliminated from an AAU tournament.

Section IV — Final Thoughts

The 2006-07 UT basketball season was a historic one, and this team has raised the bar for Tennessee hoops. For me, it has been an incredible journey, and I have been blessed to live and share my childhood dream with all of you. Even in the agony of defeat, I wouldn't trade my position with anyone.

Basketball, a simple game, has had an impact on my life that I could never have imagined. I have made life-long friendships with people whose paths I would never have crossed if it weren't for our common interest of basketball. Through the self discipline basketball has required from me, my relationship with the Lord has benefitted. Basketball has allowed me to represent the loyalty, work ethic, and dedication of my family and my University on a national stage. Basketball has provided the greatest times in my life and opened up so many opportunities that wouldn't be possible if it weren't for this great sport.

Although our team came up a few games short of the ultimate collegiate basketball goal—winning a national championship, I was rewarded with success. It doesn't always work out this way. Earlier in this book I used one of my favorite quotes, "The harder you work, the luckier you get." But I'll steal a refinement of this quote which is one of my favorite Bruce Pearl quotes and write, "Hard work won't guarantee you success, but I'll guarantee you that you won't have success without hard work." All I can say to aspiring players, is that in whatever sport you play never cheat the game. Give all you can to the game and if it isn't enough then you can walk away with your head held high knowing you did everything possible to achieve your goals. I guess losing never gets any easier. But, in my final game, I can't tell you how comforting it was to know that I couldn't go any harder for the last time around because I had been going as hard as I could all along.

If it wasn't meant to be then it wasn't meant to be, but hold up your end of the deal by doing your level best. The even greater challenge for all of us is to try and apply this philosophy to everything we do in life.

Every facet of our team is an extension of Coach Pearl's work, vision, philosophy, energy, charisma and positive, caring attitude. A friend of Coach Pearl's asked me to write a letter about what Coach Pearl has meant to me. I felt it necessary to share this letter which follows:

Original Letter to Coach Bruce Pearl

It's impossible to put into words what Coach Pearl has meant to me, but I will do my best. He brought life to a basketball program and revitalized all the players, fans and supporters involved. As a player, I feel fortunate that I was still around for this process. I had worked so hard my whole life to get to the Division I level, yet couldn't even enjoy the game I loved. Coach Pearl enabled me to live out my dream as I had envisioned as a child and allowed us all to enjoy the game, again. It is too easy to say that winning cures all. Even in defeat, I would rather have been on Coach Pearl's side because I knew that we did everything we could possibly have done to win.

In two years, Coach Pearl has brought so much joy to those involved with the Tennessee program and the Knoxville community. What makes him so special is that the biggest thrill and reward for him is bringing joy to others. It's never about him; it is about the smile on the faces of players during the celebration of victory in the locker room. Everyone knows what a brilliant basketball coach he is, but it would be an insult if all I talked about was the "on court" impact Coach has had on my life.

I have developed a bond and made a life-long friend with my head coach. Those who are unfamiliar with the average player/coach relationship in college athletics don't understand how rare this is. I can proudly say that no college athlete will walk away from his/her program with more admiration and respect for their head coach than I will. I speak for everyone on our team; from All-American to walk-ons.

If we had more people with Coach Pearl's heart in college basketball, the profession would greatly benefit. However, an even greater compliment is that if we had more people with Coach Pearl's heart in our society, our world would greatly benefit. His work ethic, loyalty, passion and faith are respected by all. I am truly blessed to have had Coach Pearl come into my life, as he brought significance to my career and opened up more "post college" opportunities than I could ever have imagined. Thank you, Coach Pearl, for making the game I love fun again. More importantly, thank you for your friendship.

Dane

§§§

You have been a part of the 2006-07 Tennessee Volunteers basketball season and have an inside view of it all. You have experienced the early morning workouts, the sacrifices, the road trips, inside the locker room, the personalities, the worries of a college athlete, the academic demands, the thrill of victory, and the agony of defeat. Most of all, you have experienced the blood, sweat and tears.

Postscript
(Some of the Facts)

As any serious Tennessee sports fan knows, UT's men's basketball success throughout the history of our great University has been limited. Table 1 illustrates this by showing that since records have been kept, starting in 1908, only 20 teams have won 20 or more games in a season's competition. Coach Ray Mears' teams had seven of these successful campaigns, Coach Don DeVoe had six, and Coach Jerry Green had four. In his first two seasons at UT, Coach Pearl already has led his teams to two of these successful campaigns. Another major barometer of a successful Division I season is postseason NCAA Tournament play. As Table 1 further illustrates, Coach Pearl, with a UT record of three wins and two losses, is the only UT basketball men's coach in the school's history with a winning postseason NCAA record. Overall, in his 15 years as a collegiate head coach, Pearl owns a 21-11 career record in NCAA Tournament play.

No one can foretell the future, but with Coach Pearl at the helm, the future of UT's men's basketball team looks very bright.

For the 2006-07 season, the official UT team record was 24 wins and 11 losses. The 24 wins are the second-most in school history. Table 2 lists each of these games and the final scores. Only the 1999-2000 team won more games (26) in a season.

Some other team highlights include (1) Tennessee is 29-2 at Thompson-Boling Arena over the last two seasons; (2) The Vols are 15-0 in non-conference home games under Coach Bruce Pearl and (3) UT's home attendance of 19,661 this season is the second-largest average in school history. The record is 20,823 in 1987-88, the first year Thompson-Boling Arena was open.

Table 3 shows our complete 2006-07 coaching staff and team roster with some key player statistics and information, including hometowns. Chris Lofton led the SEC in scoring, was selected the SEC Player of the Year and was named an All-American. I'll never be remembered as a guy who rewrote the record books. However, maybe to some peoples' surprise, I finished my career in the Top 10 of all-time at UT in the following categories: Third in season steals (67), fifth in career steals (162) ninth in career assists (386), and tied for eighth in career games played (124). During my final season, I ranked second in the SEC in assist-to-turnover ratio per game (2.82), third in steals per game (1.97) and seventh in assists per game (4.74).

All of the information in these tables was provided by Tennessee Sports Information, website UTsports.com.

Table 1
Successful UT Basketball Teams

Two widely accepted measurements of a successful season in Division I collegiate basketball are (1) winning 20 or more victories and (2) selection to compete in the NCAA postseason tournament. Of course, elite teams are also measured by their ability to win in NCAA postseason play. This is a tabulation of such successful teams throughout UT's history.

Season	Won-Lost Record	Coach
1947-48	20 wins, 5 losses	Emmett Lowery
1964-65	20 wins, 5 losses	Ray Mears
1966-67	20 wins, 6 losses	Ray Mears
1967-68	21 wins, 7 losses	Ray Mears* (0-1)
1968-69	21 wins, 7 losses	Ray Mears
1970-71	21 wins, 7 losses	Ray Mears
1975-76	21 wins, 6 losses	Ray Mears* (0-1)
1976-77	22 wins, 6 losses	Ray Mears* (0-1)
1978-79	21 wins, 12 losses	Don DeVoe* (1-1)
1980-81	21 wins, 8 losses	Don DeVoe** (1-1)
1981-82	20 wins, 10 losses	Don DeVoe* (1-1)
1982-83	20 wins, 12 losses	Don DeVoe* (1-1)
1983-84	21 wins, 14 losses	Don DeVoe
1984-85	22 wins, 15 losses	Don DeVoe
1997-98	20 wins, 9 losses	Jerry Green* (0-1)
1998-99	21 wins, 9 losses	Jerry Green*(1-1)
1999-2000	26 wins, 7 losses	Jerry Green** (2-1)
2000-01	22 wins, 11 losses	Jerry Green* (0-1)
2005-06	22 wins, 8 losses	Bruce Pearl* (1-1)
2006-07	24 wins, 11 losses	Bruce Pearl** (2-1)

* Team selected to play in NCAA Tournament. The numbers in parenthesis are the NCAA Tournament won-lost record (wins-losses).
** Team selected to play in NCAA Tournament and advanced to Sweet 16.

Table 2
2006-07 Tennessee Vol Basketball Results

DATE	OPPONENT	SCORE	ATTEND
11/10/06	MIDDLE TENNESSEE	W 83-52	17798
11/13/06	Fordham	W 78-71	3186
11/14/06	UNC-Wilmington	W 87-75	3351
11/19/06	COPPIN STATE	W 99-65	21633
11/22/06	Butler	44-56 L	9123
11/24/06	North Carolina	87-101 L	9498
11/27/06	at Louisiana-Lafayette	W 77-67	4364
12/01/06	MURRAY STATE	W 89-64	16807
12/06/06	MEMPHIS	W 76-58	19714
12/16/06	WESTERN KENTUCKY	W 93-79	17895
12/18/06	Oklahoma State	W 79-77	8118
12/23/06	TEXAS	W 111-105(ot)	20778
12/28/06	TENNESSEE TECH	W 101-77	19001
12/30/06	EAST TENNESSEE STATE	W 93-88	18216
01/07/07	MISSISSIPPI STATE	W 92-84	17603
01/10/07*	at Vanderbilt	81-82 L	14316
01/13/07	Ohio State	66-68 L	18817
01/17/07*	at Auburn	80-83 L	8271
01/20/07*	SOUTH CAROLINA	W 64-61	23238
01/24/07*	at Ole Miss	69-83 L	8052
01/28/07*	at Kentucky	57-76 L	24311
01/31/07*	GEORGIA	W 82-71	17686
02/03/07*	at University of Florida	78-94 L	12222
02/06/07*	LSU	W 70-67	17274
02/10/07*	VANDERBILT	W 84-57	21493
02/13/07*	KENTUCKY	W 89-85	22320
02/17/07*	at South Carolina	64-81 L	12789
02/21/07*	ALABAMA	W 69-66(ot)	19068
02/24/07*	at Arkansas	W 83-72	18903
02/27/07*	FLORIDA	W 86-76	24047
03/03/07*	at Georgia Bulldogs	W 71-65	10230
03/08/07*	LSU	67-76 L(ot)	14574
03/16/07	Long Beach State	W 121-86	19916
03/18/07	Virginia	W 77-74	19916
03/22/07	Ohio State	84-85 L	26776

* - SEC games
Home games are denoted by capital letters

VERTICAL LEAP

Table 3 - 2006-07 Player & Coaching Staff Information

Player	GP	Min/G	FG%	3Pt%	FT%	R/G	A/G	Stl	B	Pts/G
Lofton, Chris	31	29.6	.479	.419	.811	3.1	1.7	45	4	20.8
Smith, JaJuan	35	28.9	.455	.368	.729	4.5	1.3	73	8	15.2
Smith, Ramar	35	27.2	.437	.310	.662	3.3	3.1	40	9	10.7
Chism, Wayne	35	19.4	.441	.329	.587	5.2	0.9	21	21	9.1
Crews, Duke	35	19.8	.518	.000	.577	5.1	0.6	22	32	8.4
Childress, Ryan	35	15.7	.457	.375	.565	4.0	0.8	22	14	5.6
Bradshaw, Dane	35	27.5	.348	.290	.550	4.0	4.7	67	14	5.5
Howell, Jordan	27	18.3	.351	.346	.684	1.3	1.5	12	0	3.9
Tabb, Josh	35	17.6	.500	.302	.385	2.8	1.1	30	2	3.5
Johnson, Marques	4	11.3	.250	.333	.600	0.5	1.3	1	0	2.0
Passley, Tony	17	6.8	.393	.250	.500	1.7	0.5	2	3	1.8
Cannington, Quinn	5	1.0	1.00	1.00	.000	0.0	0.0	0	0	0.6
Wild, Tanner	10	1.3	.200	.500	.000	0.1	0.1	0	0	0.3
Daniels-Mulholland, R	3	1.0	.000	.000	.000	0.0	0.0	0	0	0.0
Jackson, Justin	1	2.0	.000	.000	.000	0.0	0.0	0	0	0.0
Bosse, Ben	9	1.9	.000	.000	.000	0.2	0.1	1	1	0.0
Total	35		.448	.365	.653	35.8	15.6	336	108	80.9

No.	Name	Pos.	Ht.	Wt.	Cl.	Hometown
2	Smith, JaJuan	G	6-2	196	Jr.	Cleveland, Tennessee
4	Chism, Wayne	F	6-9	245	Fr.	Bolivar, Tennessee
5	Lofton, Chris	G	6-2	200	Jr.	Maysville, Kentucky
11	Cannington, Quinn	G	6-4	165	Fr.	Knoxville, Tennessee
12	Smith, Ramar	G	6-2	185	Fr.	Mt. Clemens, Michigan
13	Passley, Tony	F	6-5	218	So.	Indianapolis, Indiana
15	Howell, Jordan	G	6-3	192	Jr.	Auburn, Alabama
21	Jackson, Justin	G	5-11	173	So.	Fredericksburg, Virginia
22	Pearl, Steven	F	6-5	222	Fr.	Knoxville, Tennessee
23	Bradshaw, Dane	G/F	6-4	205	Sr.	Memphis, Tennessee
24	Wild, Tanner	G	6-0	170	So.	Huntington, West Va.
25	Tabb, Josh	G	6-4	193	Fr.	Carbondale, Illinois
30	Bosse, Ben	F	6-7	197	So.	Knoxville, Tennessee
32	Crews, Duke	F	6-7	233	Fr.	Hampton, Virginia
34	Childress, Ryan	F	6-9	238	So.	Cincinnati, Ohio
40	Daniels-Mulholland, R	F	6-5	250	So.	Oak Ridge, Tennessee

Head Coach: Bruce Pearl (Boston College, 1982)
Associate Head Coach: Tony Jones (Concordia University, 1993)
Assistant Coach: Steve Forbes (Southern Arkansas, 1988)
Assistant Coach: Jason Shay (Iowa, 1995)
Director of Operations: Ken Johnson (Albertson College, 1993)
Basketball Trainer: Chad Newman (Tennessee, 1994)
Strength Coach: Troy Wills (Emory & Henry, 2000)

Photograph Gallery

Photographs are wonderful complements to any story, as they can convey feelings and detail impossible to describe with words. There are so many great UT photographs available it was difficult to choose the best ones to share in my photograph gallery. However, from my perspective, I believe the one's selected capture the essence of our season. Many of these photographs are from my family or my own personal collection, but the majority were provided by Elizabeth Olivier, UTSports. com. Thank you, Elizabeth. Credit lines are shown for each of Elizabeth's photographs.

Together!

Josh Tabb fitting in just fine at the party.

Nothin' like spending Saturday morning with Troy Wills and
25 lb. weight vests doing stadium sprints at Neyland Stadium.

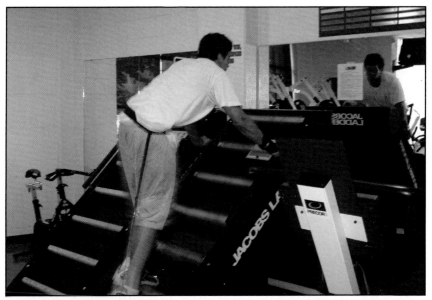

A good look at the Jacobs Ladder.

The rubber duckies help keep your mind off the
dreadfully cold temperature in the whirlpool.

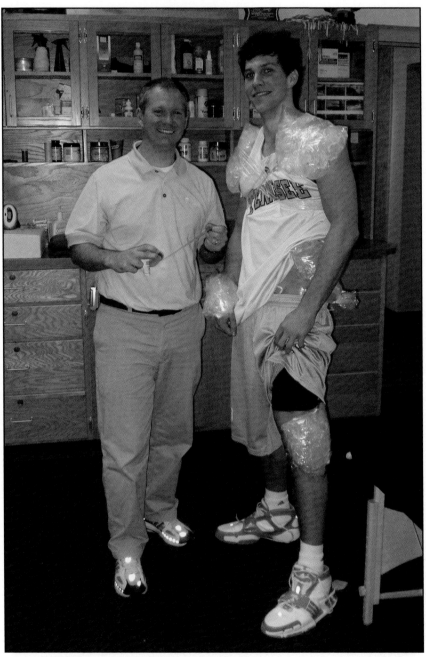

I didn't make Chad Newman's job any easier throughout my four years.

The team in front of Rockefeller Center.

Above: As you can see, Chris Lofton's face shows how thrilled he is to be taking a picture.

Left: Tony Passley and me on the streets of New York City.

ESPN Analyst, Stacey Dales, is one of many sports celebs I met in New York.

Elizabeth Olivier / UTSports.com

The managers set us up nicely in our locker room at MSG.

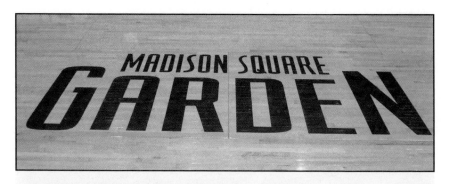

JaJuan Smith holds Steve Francis' shoe in front of his locker.

Soaking it all in at Madison Square Garden.

Above: Wayne Chism puts fear in all the passengers as he enters the cockpit.

Left: Ben Bosse is in "deep thought" during study hall on the road.

Elizabeth Olivier / UTSports.com

What a thrill! Entering through the student
section, proves there is no place like home.

The starting five communicating on the court.

All eyes and ears are on Coach Pearl, as he instructs during a time-out.

Elizabeth Olivier / UTSports.com

Getting into the lane
on our way to a big
win against the
Memphis Tigers.

Elizabeth Olivier / UTSports.com

Great visual evidence
that Coach Pearl and I
are on the same page.

Getting fired up in the "players-only" huddle, after the line-ups are announced.

Our fast paced style is something all of our players enjoy.

Coach Pearl brings his intensity and passion every day.

Not sure how many coaches exchange chest bumps
with their players, but Bruce Pearl does.

Living up to his reputation, Coach Pearl uses my jersey
to wipe the sweat from his face.

Being interviewed by my man,
Jimmy Dykes, after
the game winning tip-in
vs. Oklahoma State.

Elizabeth Olivier / UTSports.com

It may not be worth much, but I get to as many autograph requests as I can.

Elizabeth Olivier / UTSports.com

I was embraced by
my parents after the
Oklahoma State game.

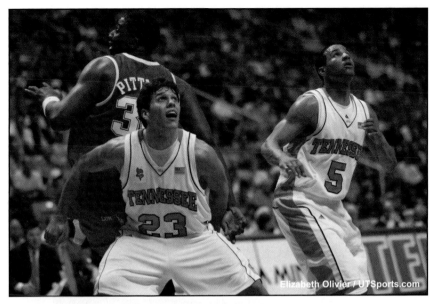

Above: Doing my best
to keep the taller, bigger
opponent off the glass.

Most likely the first
and last time I will have
a picture of me taking on the
National Player of the Year,
Kevin Durant.

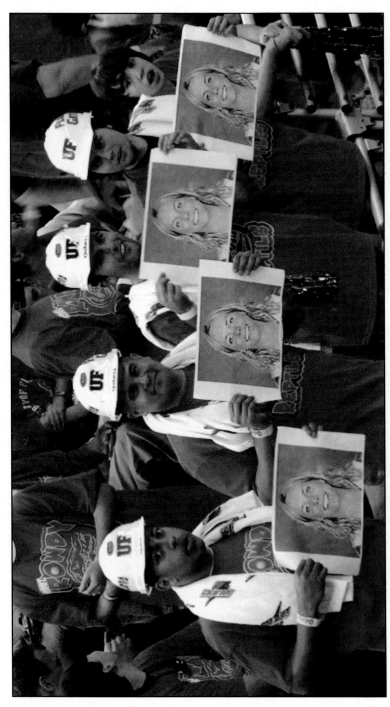

Photos of my sister, Bridget, were passed throughout the Florida student section as they chanted "Bridget's Better!"

Trying to see the whole floor as I push the ball up the court.

The streamers came down from the ceiling, after beating Kentucky at home for the first time in my career.

The coaches and I celebrate with "Ernie & Bernie"
after a huge win at home over Kentucky.

Left to right: Ernie Grunfield, Dane and Bernard King.

Left to right: Ernie Grunfield, Bruce Pearl, Tony Jones,
Bernard King and Ken Johnson

For the love of Dane Bradshaw and Tennessee Basketball, please leave The Rock painted until after the game.

The students provided me the most memorable Senior Night I could have imagined. (The Rock, "Dane-Train" and celebrating in the student section.)

The announcement was made that Coach Pearl generously
endowed a $100,000 scholarship in my name.

It was great to have my whole family in town to share in this special moment.

I'll definitely miss playing in front of the
sellout crowds in Thompson-Boling Arena.

My final exit off "The Summitt" floor. Thank you Knoxville!

Celebrating with the students after a big
win versus Florida, capped off a heck of a Senior night.

Bob Kesling (*right*) and Bert Bertelkamp (*left*) played
huge roles in making it a special four years for me.

Elizabeth Olivier / UTSports.com

This wasn't exactly the plan when I decided to penetrate into the lane against
LSU's Glen "Big Baby" Davis, 6'9", 290 lbs. and Magnum Rolle, 6'10".

We all celebrate together as our name is announced on Selection Sunday.

Left to right: Mark Pancratz, Mark Fogle, Andrew Channiot, (me) and Brooks Savage. The best graduate assistant and managers in the country.

Converting a layup as we cruised past Long Beach State in Round 1 of the NCAA Tournament.

This was a big play for us versus Virginia as I won the battle for the loose ball.

Elizabeth Olivier / UTSports.com

Virginia was forced to call a time-out after we regained momentum.

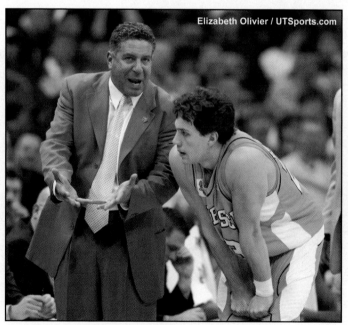

Elizabeth Olivier / UTSports.com

I don't remember, but I'm pretty sure I had
just done something wrong.

The bench stormed the court as the buzzer sounded,
officially putting us into the Sweet 16.

Chris and I are all smiles after advancing to the Sweet 16.

Top left: Lifelong friend, Derek Clenin, and I hold up our 10 and under championship trophy. We went 48-0. *Top right:* Needless to say, this was before the Scottie Pippen Camp. *Below:* The Maui Invitational was a tournament my family definitely didn't mind traveling to in 2004.